Smart Traveler's Zealand – Fro... Perspective

A Budget Friendly Guide for What to See, Where to Go, Where to Stay, What to Eat, National Parks, Famous Movie Landmarks & MORE!

Sophia Taylor

Copyright © 2022 by Galicia Publishing House.

All Rights Reserved.

No part of the book may be reproduced, stored in a retrieval system or transmitted, in any form or by any means, without the prior written authorization of the publisher, except as permitted under the United States Copyright Act of 1976.

While the author and the publisher have made every effort to verify information here, neither the author nor the publisher assumes any responsibility for errors in, omission from or a different interpretation of the subject matter. The reader assumes all responsibility for the use of the information.

Published by: Galicia Publishing House

Support@BarberryBooks.com

Design & Cover by Angella Sitompul

First Edition

Contents

Introduction 7

A Brief History of New Zealand 14

Languages – Slang & Other Idiosyncrasies 18

When to Visit and Costs 23

    The Best Time to Visit 23

    Costs of a Budget Trip to New Zealand 24

    Trip Budget 29

Things to Know before you Go 31

    Immigration 31

    Currency & Exchange Rate 32

    Electric Plugs & Voltage 33

    Health Care 33

    Accident Compensation (ACC) 34

    What to Pack 34

    What Not to Pack 38

    Digital Pack List 39

Typical Food & Drink of New Zealand 41

Transport Options 45

Hire a Campervan 45

Modes of Public Transport 46

Play, Stay, Do & See 49

Day 1 & 2: Auckland 50

Day 3 -6: Bay of Islands & Cape Reinga 55

Day 7 – 10: Coromandel & Rotorua 59

Rotorua 63

Day 11-13:Taupo & Napier 67

Napier 73

Day 14 & 17: Wellington & Wairarapa 77

Martinborough 84

South Island 87

Day 18-20: Marlborough & Kaikoura 88

Day 20 – 21: The West Coast 92

Day 22 – 24: Queenstown & Wanaka 96

Day 25: Milford Sound & Te Anau 102

Day 26 – 27: Southland & Stewart Island 103

Day 28 – 29: The Catlins & Dunedin 108

Day 30 – 32: Lake Tekapo & Christchurch 112

Alternative Cost-Effective Ways to see New Zealand on a Budget *118*

    Airbnb 118

    Housesitting 119

    Budget Motels 120

    Work for Trade 120

Sustainability & You (The Tourist).. 122

    Green Energy Accommodation 125

    Background of NZ's Sustainability 126

Crime & Safety.. 131

Undiscovered Gems & Off the Beaten Track 138

    Taranaki (New Plymouth) 138

    Waitomo Caves.. 141

    Otorohanga Kiwi House 143

    South Island Gem... 143

    Holiday Accommodation.. 147

        School Cottage 147

        Little Colonsay Beach House 149

        Gunyah.. 151

Hunting & Fishing Seasons 158

Fishing Regulations *161*

Preparing & Cooking Fish & Shellfish *163*

New Zealand's National Parks *166*

Tongariro National Park *167*

    Tongariro Alpine Crossing 167

    Tongariro Northern Circuit 4 Days 41 km 168

    Round the Mountain Track 6 Days, 66.2 km 170

    Nature Trails 173

    Waterfalls 173

    Skiing 173

    New Zealand's Highest Café (Highly Recommended by a Local) 174

    Lord of the Rings Film Sites 174

Able Tasman National Park *175*

Aoraki Mount Cook National Park *179*

    Mountain Walks 180

    Glacier Viewing and Skiing 180

    Mountaineering 181

    Accommodation 181

Conclusion *183*

Introduction

As the world re-awakens from the Covid 19 border closures, the travel bug begins to bite again. It's time to take that bucket list trip of a lifetime. You know you have always wanted to do it. New Zealand, where adventures abound.

You can have a fantastic time on a budget. It helps to

know what you are doing. So let this local guide you through the most picturesque, lean, green country in the world.

We are perched in the South Pacific Ocean; about 1600 kilometres to the northwest is our closest neighbour, Australia. New Zealand is divided into two main Islands. The North Island and The South Island.

New Zealand (Aotearoa, in the indigenous Māori) has been my home for 58 years, not counting the three years I lived in Melbourne, Australia. Every Australian remarked on my New Zealand accent while I lived there. That's not why I came back, by the way. I felt like a trained seal at times as they wanted me to say various words and phrases they found hilarious.

So, I became a walking travel ambassador for New Zealand. 'Have you ever been to New Zealand?' I would ask unsuspecting punters. It's surprising how many said, 'No' 'It's a country everyone needs to visit at least once in their lives.' I told them. I got a couple of takers who did come without letting me know and came back wide-eyed at how expensive it was. 'Well, if you had told me before you went, I could have told you how to visit New Zealand on a budget.'

As we travel through this guide, I will give you a history lesson, introduce some fun facts, and teach you how to sound like a local. Tell you the best times to go for the activities you want to do and show you sights and sounds and tastes you can sample on a budget. Stick with me, and I will show you how to live like a king in some of the best surroundings in the world.

Starting from Cape Reinga in the North and finishing at Stewart Island in the South, you will be guided through everything from transport to accommodation. There is always room for a splurge or two on vacation, so the nightlife of the regions is highlighted as must-do and-see items. Perhaps a one- or two-night stay in luxury accommodation will satisfy a splurge, or dinners in revolving restaurants, shows, and live concerts will give you fabulous memories to take home.

There is so much to see and do that one trip would not do it justice. So, I have chosen the gold from our New Zealand crown.

So, let's start with 15 fun and quirky facts:

1. We are the first country in the world to see the sunrise, although this is considered a controversial fact, as technically Samoa lays claim to this. Due to the way the earth curves, the North Island city of Gisborne on the East Coast is the first to see the sunrise.

2. God Save the Queen is an official anthem of New Zealand. In fact, we have two, 'God of Nations' is sung before rugby matches both here and at overseas games.

3. We were the first country to give women the vote in 1893. An iconic New Zealand figure, Kate Shepard, who worked with the women's suffragettes, gathered 30,000 signatures for Parliament led to women gaining the right to vote. In addition, we have a female Prime Minister, Jacinda Ardern, who is world-famous for her Covid 19 stance and Governor General, Dame Cindy Kiro, who was sworn in on the 21st of September 2021.

4. We conquered Everest and discovered the proton. Discovering the proton was news to me, but even at home, you learn something new every day. According to history, a gentleman by the name of Sir Earnest Rutherford in 1919.

5. We have the longest place name in the world, it is:

Taumatawhakatangi-Hangakoauauotamatea-Pokaiwhenuakitanatanatahu which is the name of a 300-meter-high hill in the fruit capital, Hawkes Bay. It has 40 syllables which is a bit of a tongue twister by any stretch of the imagination. If trying to pronounce it does you head in, just shorten it to Taumata. The locals will know what you are talking about.

6. We are a hotbed of volcanoes. Our part of the earth is called the Pacific Ring of Fire, and I don't mean the bathroom kind. Mt Ruapehu is still classed as an active volcano, and our biggest city, Auckland, is built on a large volcanic field of 53 volcanoes. These have lain dormant for the last 500 years.

7. We have the clearest waters in the world, and that's not just tooting our own horn. It's true. The Blue Lake in the Nelson Lakes National park holds the world record for the clearest water, with a visibility of 80 metres.

8. Our insects are big; generally, we don't have the poisonous wildlife of Australia, but we have some impressive specimens.

A native to our land is the Weta, the largest insect in the world. With ears on its knees, it loves carrots and weighs 70 grams. I have lived here all my life and never seen one, so the chances of seeing one are nil. So don't panic. If you want to panic about wildlife, go to Australia, they eat you over there or kill you with toxins. I never saw anything sinister over there in the 3 years I lived there.

9. Our birds were large when the Moa was running around; it stood at 3.6 metres and weighed a healthy 230 kilos. However, these giants are now extinct. Our iconic Kiwi is a very small flightless bird who lives in dark environments and only comes out at night to feed.

10. Our Dolphins are cute, small, and friendly. They jump and play in the harbours of Wellington and Picton, often seen leaping alongside the ferry as it crosses from the North Island to the South Island. They populate many of the coastal areas around New Zealand.

11. A land of 40 million sheep. Agriculture is a huge industry here, and most of these sheep go out as exports, so you would think we can get cheap lamb here. Not, so, we pay up to $26 a kilo. You can get cheaper New Zealand lamb anywhere but here. Weird!

12. And a lot of cars, about 2.5 million of them, which is strange given we have a people population of 5.5 million

and not all those people drive or can drive. Getting around by car is a popular choice in New Zealand; you can tell by the number of cars on the road.

13. Plenty of butter and cheese, which again makes one wonder why butter is $7.00 a block when so much of it is exported. New Zealand cheese is wonderful, the rest of the world agrees, but we still pay $14 a kilo for cheese.

Then there are the fancy pants cheeses you can enjoy on a cheese and fruit platter in Tapas Bars or as an after-dinner finish instead of dessert.

14. We are huge Star Wars fans, huge! Proving this by watching the movies over and over and over and talking about them long after the curtain falls. Even our Universities use them in literature courses

15. Hobbits Rule, unless you have been living under a rock somewhere, you will know New Zealand was the film location for 'The Lord of the Rings' Our very own Sir Peter Jackson was the filmmaker, and it was a massive project that took 275 days of shooting over 150 locations with 300+ sets.

A Brief History of New Zealand

The tribes of the Far-North (Ngapuhi) say the first explorer to reach New Zealand was the Polynesian navigator, Kupe. The first settlers after him arrived from Hawaiki between 1200 and 1300 AD. They discovered New Zealand by navigating the ocean currents, the wind, and the stars.

New Zealand was the last large and livable place to be discovered and therefore is the youngest country in terms of human settlement. Able Tasman, a Dutch explorer, was the next to see New Zealand from his set in 1642. Our country began as 'Nieuw Zeeland, 'which comes from the

Dutch mapmakers of the time. This is the origin of the name 'New Zealand.

127 years later, Englishman Captain James Cook arrived on the first of three voyages to New Zealand, followed by European whalers and sealers, followed by traders.

Early in the 1930s, the British government wanted to reduce drunkenness and lawlessness so they could settle here before the French, who were eyeing New Zealand up as a potential home.

Fast forward to 6 February 1840 and the signing of the Treaty of Waitangi, an agreement between the British and Māori settling how they could live side by side peacefully. The British, later, reneged on the Treaty badly, as you will see in later land wars. The basis of which fuels Treaty grievances still to be settled today.

William Hobson, New Zealand's first Governor, invited all the Māori Chiefs around the country to sign the Treaty with the British crown.

As the Treaty travelled around the country with William Hobson over 500 Māori Chiefs signed it. Today it is known as the Treaty of Waitangi (Te Tiriti o Waitangi).

After the signing, Māori came under much pressure from the European settlers to sell their land which had not been agreed to in the signing of the Treaty.

A lot of Māori land was forcibly taken or swapped for blankets and medicines in lieu of payment during the 20 years of land wars. This was predominantly in the North Island.

In the meantime, the South Island settled well, with settlers starting sheep farms on the flat grass lands of Canterbury.

Canterbury became the wealthiest region, especially when gold was discovered in Otago in 1861 and then again on the West Coast of the South Island. These gold finds helped put Dunedin on the map as the largest city in New Zealand at that time.

The first exports of meat, cheese and butter started in 1882. Following on from the success of the first exports, New Zealand became the biggest supplier to Britain. Much of the New Zealand economy was based on agriculture and Forestry.

As the war years continued, thousands of New Zealand soldiers fought and died overseas in the First World War. The tradition of ANZAC (Australian and New Zealand Army Corps) thus forms a special relationship with Australia.

Today this relationship between Australia and New Zealand has deteriorated, and the tradition of ANZAC is no longer honoured as a special relationship. Australia has harsher rules for Kiwis in Australia whereas New Zealand has an open-door policy for Australian citizens.

New Zealand gained independence as a nation in the 1890s. Instead of joining the Australian Federation, New Zealand became an independent Dominion in 1907.

There are seven ethnic groups that make up New Zealand. European, Māori, Pacific peoples, Middle Eastern, African, Indian, and Asian.

This breaks down to 25% of people in New Zealand were born overseas, 15% are Māori, over 12% are Asian, and 7% are from the Island Nations.

Languages – Slang & Other Idiosyncrasies

How to blend in with the rest of the Natives in New Zealand depends on how much you sound like the locals. If, however, you are planning a trip to New Zealand outside of your language barrier, be sure to select the best language App for your trip.

For everyone else, follow me through for the most important words and phrases and colloquialisms you will need to know.

Ki Ora is a greeting in the Māori language. It means

'Hello,' 'Thank you,' and 'Well done.'

Aotearoa is New Zealand in the Māori. It means land of the long white cloud. If you visit Egmont National Park, you will see the cloud over Mt Taranaki.

"Sweet as" is a phrase that means 'awesome' or 'thank you.'

Choice is a word that means 'cool' or 'I agree.'

Chur means 'thanks'; you may also hear 'ta' for 'thanks.'

Bring a plate means to bring food to share a meal. Nothing cracks us Kiwis up more than when foreigners make the mistake of bringing an empty plate.

My shout/Your shout, this phase means my shout I'm going to pay for the meal or drinks, your shout means you pay

Yeah, Nah, is how we say 'thanks but no thanks'

The Dairy is another name for 'convenience store.'

Tramping means hiking

Bach refers to 'holiday home.'

Gumboots means rubber boots worn on the farm

She'll be right means 'everything will be okay.'

Bench refers to a table or bench in the kitchen

Across the Ditch refers to Australia, and in Australia, this refers to New Zealand

Chilly Bin carries drinks or food to the beach while keeping them cool

Jandals, typically worn at the beach, another name for them is Flip Flops

Cuppa means, 'would you like a cup of tea.'

Togs, if someone says to bring you togs, it means bathing suit, you are going swimming

Chook, this refers to a chicken; many Kiwis have their own to cut food costs and live an eco-friendlier life

JAFA means Just another f*ck*ng Aucklander, a derogatory term meaning people from Auckland are considered snobs. The friends and family I know there are wonderful.

Aroha means Love

Pakeha means white people

Koha, this is one of my favourites in Te Reo (The Language). It means gift or donation

Kai means food

Kai Moana Kai means food, and moana means sea; together, it means food from the sea

Whanau means blood-related or good friends, family

Marae is a gathering place for Māori, a shared but sacred space. They hold meetings, tangi (funerals), celebrations and church services in this space. There are proper protocols for coming onto the Marae, greeting, meeting, and eating. For large events like tangi, people sleep overnight in the Meeting house. You must never enter the meeting house with footwear on

Mana refers to the strength and integrity of your soul and your values. It can also mean power, authority, and reputation

Mahi is the word for work. Means 'do the work' 'go to work.'

Hongi is a customary Māori greeting where people rub noses

Kapai means 'well done' or that you have impressed someone

This list is by no means complete. It contains a few of the most common words you are likely to hear on your trip. If you need a more complete language app, source one before you come or bring a dictionary with all the place names and words you will need.

The nuances of slang words and phrases can leave your mind boggled. I'm a local, and it took me time to learn the lingo. Don't panic; you will be fine.

When to Visit and Costs

The Best Time to Visit

This will depend on what activities you want to do on your trip. There is no use bringing skis in the Summer because there is no snow on the mountains. In Winter, it's okay to bring swimming gear to relax in Thermal Hot Springs, don't expect to go swimming in the ocean or rivers or lakes unless you want your unmentionables up behind your ears. This is how cold it is.

Autumn and Spring are the in-between seasons, when festivals, agricultural shows and other major events are held. Each region has its various Autumn and Spring programmes to show case the best of what their region has to offer.

Depending on what you plan to see and do first, you land at the international airport closest to your desired destination. For example, Auckland International Airport for the top and middle of the North Island.

Wellington International Airport for the middle and lower North Island and to connect with the InterIslander ferry from North Island to South Island. Christchurch International Airport to take in the South Island sights.

Costs of a Budget Trip to New Zealand

For many travellers, a trip to New Zealand is a bucket list dream. Choosing an itinerary will be hard when you are spoiled for choice. There are so many experiences, stunning sights, and adventures to be had. Everyone talks about the tourist attractions, adventure sports and sightseeing tours.

For a trip to New Zealand, you must be willing to save and bear the cost, especially if it is a trip of a lifetime.

New Zealand is expensive, I won't lie about that, but it can be done on a budget.

The cost of flights will set you back between $1700-2300 and does not include the cost of visas and passports. Always book and pay for your flights and travel documents at least 6 months in advance; this way, everything you need to fly will be covered. Don't forget the travel insurance. If you can't afford travel insurance, you can't afford to travel.

The budget set out is for a 35-day trip, excluding your flights because you have already taken care of those details with savings, extra hours at work or via side hustling extra money to reach your goal faster.

A year beforehand, decide your savings goal. Saving $10,000 in a year means you will need to save $200.00 per week. After paying for your flights and associated costs, this leaves you a budget of $6000 to enjoy 35 days in New Zealand.

The cost of the roof over your head is the biggest outlay of your trip unless you have friends in New Zealand or work for accommodation. These opportunities mean your costs will be lower but not altogether eliminated as you travel to other parts of the country.

The average cost of a night of backpackers accommodation is $50 a night, which will consume at least the first $1,100 of your $6,000 budget. Assuming you pay for accommodation for the entire time you are here, you are looking at $1050.00. The best sites to book accommodation are Hostel World, Airbnb or Booking.com.

Filling your tummy is easy, providing you don't eat every meal out. Small piece of advice here, Don't! You can't afford to starve. Cooking most of your meals will save you mega bucks.

Eggs, porridge or Weetbix for breakfast with milk and a banana. Sandwiches for lunch. Fruit, nuts or popcorn for snacks and pasta or stir-fry for dinner. If you stick to a basic diet like this, you will be able to keep your grocery bill to around $250.00 for the whole trip.

Keep eating out once or twice a week if you are with friends or just to splurge for one or two evenings out over the course of your holiday. You do get to eat out; just keep it to a minimum. Allow $400 for eating out. If alcohol is normal for you, budget this expense too. Keep the budget to $70.00-80.00 just so you can sample some New Zealand wines. Wine is award-winning in New Zealand, so even the house wine is an excellent choice.

Transport is another cost that can add up quickly if you don't find cheaper options. If the thought of driving in New Zealand fills you with anxiety at driving on the left-hand side of the road, then maybe this is not the best option for you. Hiring a camper van is costly with hire age, bond, insurance, fuel, and camping site fees. It might feel cheaper with accommodation all rolled into the deal, but the costs soon add up. So, what to do?

Purchasing a flexi bus pass is the best transport option. These bus passes are hours-based travel passes designed for backpackers and independent travellers who want to experience New Zealand in their own way and time.

You can design your travel around what you want to do and see. The bus passes can be managed online, topped up to extend the hours if exploring takes longer, and bus booked anywhere at any time. These range in price from 10 hours at $98.00 to 80 hours at $561.00. Flexi- bus travel also allows you to catch the Interisland ferry and the Trans-Alpine Train. So, this is travel costs budgeted. The passes are valid for 12 months.

You can easily spend most of your budget on activities in New Zealand. There are so many things to do, and none of them budget-friendly. Allow $600.00 - $700 for things to do and then you can have two big-ticket adventures and still have change for smaller activities. Adrenaline junkies can take on thrill-seeking activities such as bungee jumping or sky diving.

Outdoors lovers can hike or walk trails for free. However, a cruise through Milford Sound and swimming with the dolphins, even though expensive, are totally worth it. For a Milford Sound day cruise with lunch included, be prepared to part with $120.00 for 3 hours of delight.

For a cool $220.00, you can swim with the dolphins in Kaikoura. This excursion is mind-blowing and takes 3.5 hours from getting on the boat to docking back at the headquarters.

Always have a miscellaneous budget. In this instance, $200.00 in hand for items such as toiletries, sunblock, replacing the socks with a giant hole in the heel or sticking plasters to keep the blisters at bay.

Put aside $500.00 as an emergency fund; chances are

you won't have to use it, but better to be safe than sorry in case of flight delays, illness or injury or extra accommodation. Maybe a doctor's bill for that sprained ankle until you can claim on your travel insurance.

With everything included. Your entire budget for a 35-day trip to New Zealand comes to $3,720 NZD. In USD, this converts to $2,590.29, well under your allocated budget. This does not include keepsakes or other discretionary spending.

For your budget, 35 days will get you a wide range of highlights and some of the regions off the beaten track, depending on your tastes for highlights and the shape of your itinerary. Just so you know your costs up front, it helps to plan your itinerary before your trip.

Trip Budget

Here are some guidelines to keep your budget healthy throughout your trip. There is nothing worse than running out of money before you finish everything you planned.

Pack your own lunch for outdoor picnics. This is a huge

saving on cafe and takeaway food. Local supermarkets have all the food essentials for all meals. Take advantage of the cooking facilities at backpackers, as they all have self-service kitchens.

Eat the local Fish and Chips. Each region has its own version of this New Zealand quintessential takeaway. Try this meal in each region you visit.

Don't be frightened to ask for discounts and check out special deals on accommodation, transport, and activities. Tourism operators here are hungry for the tourist dollar due to the advent of Covid, so they offer some great deals on packages, like buy two get one free for accommodation. Or cut prices on popular activities.

Ask a local for directions, the time, instructions or how to catch the public transport and what the cheaper options are for using the local buses.

Travel on an Intercity Travel Pass. This is the best value for travel buck from the North to the South Island and a facility that allows you to hop on and hop off the bus to explore without being tied to a timetable.

Things to Know before you Go

Immigration

New Zealand is a breath-taking country to visit as a tourist; however, in this current Covid-19 climate, there are a few rules to be followed. You must have a negative PCR or RT-PCR test within 48 hours of departure. Both the Covid-19 sample taken and results returned within 48 hours of departure. You are responsible for the costs of your pre-departure tests.

On arrival, you will be required to produce proof of a

negative result to an official during your passport processing. There are certain items you cannot bring into the country. If you are not sure, declare it or dispose of it, particularly if it is food. Avoid a $450.00 fine. Travellers from a quarantine-free country are not required to self-isolate or enter quarantine facilities.

Advice remains to wait for borders to reopen in October 2022. Having the correct visa and a valid passport is the key to fuss-free entry into New Zealand. Waiting until October 2022 means you can enjoy a Summer holiday in beautiful New Zealand.

Currency & Exchange Rate

The New Zealand dollar is the currency of New Zealand. Exchanging currency before your trip means you can get better rates than if you were to exchange foreign cash at the airport or your hotel. Places like this are for convenience and therefore can offer the worst exchange rates. Banks usually offer the best exchange rates, and some do not charge an additional fee to exchange the currency. As part of your trip preparation, organise this beforehand.

Electric Plugs & Voltage

New Zealand's electricity runs at 230 or 240 volts. So, we use angled 2 pinned or 3 pinned plugs; this is the same as Australia or parts of Asia. Most accommodation providers provide 110-volt ac sockets for electric razors.

Health Care

Travellers from Australia have reciprocal health care agreements with the New Zealand government. This means we will treat Australian citizens for free the same as New Zealand citizens. However, it always pays to have travel health insurance cover dental or after-hours emergency doctors' visits.

The costs of the dentist in an emergency can run into hundreds of dollars. After-Hours care can cost upwards of $80 per visit with prescriptions on top at the cost of $15 per item. Some Airlines offer comprehensive travel insurance, or you could purchase it through your local health insurer.

Accident Compensation (ACC)

This is New Zealand's no-fault cover for injuries suffered because of an accident, assault, falls or mass events. It does not matter; if you are a visitor, you are covered for accidents. You will still need travel insurance for illnesses, flight delays or emergency flights back home. Your health provider will make a claim on your behalf.

What to Pack

There are essentials you must pack, no matter what. Things must be getting exciting as you get closer to the date of your trip to New Zealand. Let's look at what you need to pack no matter what for your trip.

A decent backpack is the first thing needed. Make sure you have a backpack that is the right size for you and will last the duration of your trip. Be sure to check out what to look for in a pack in the NZ Pocket Guide.

A day pack is a small, lightweight pack for carrying essentials for a day out, hiking or day trips. You only need a day pack to carry keys, phone, cash or card, a water bottle, your lunch, and a layer or two if the weather packs up.

Hiking boots or sturdy shoes are another must-have. Make sure your boots or shoes are broken in before your trip; the last thing you need is sore feet and blisters. They need to be lightweight and as waterproof as possible and fast drying. Light shoes for museum visits or night out and flip-flops for the beach.

Speaking of fast-drying, pack a fast-drying microfiber towel. It takes up less room than a normal fluffy towel. This is essential for backpacking in New Zealand.

Regardless of the season in which you are travelling in New Zealand, make sure you pack a thermal underlayer, a rain jacket, a long-sleeved hoodie, and another lightweight sweater. If you can, get yourself a merino layer as they are lightweight and warm.

A New Zealand adaptor plug is an essential need. Make sure the adaptor plug you buy has surge protection. Make sure it is small enough to pack and does not get in the way of other people's ability to plug in their appliances.

A multiplug is useful if you have a lot of devices to charge, like a camera, a phone, and a laptop. You will only need one adaptor and can use the multiplug to charge several items at once, and this takes up less room at the backpackers.

Bring some New Zealand cash, enough for two weeks of expenses, in case you have trouble with cards or you need to open a New Zealand bank account to transfer money into from home. This way, you can use a local ATM card and avoid conversion rates on your credit card.

Insect repellent for those annoying little bugs called sandflies that bite you and cause itching. They especially love beaches or picnic areas. If you are camping in a tent, this will become your new best friend.

In New Zealand, we have a giant hole in the ozone layer between New Zealand and Australia which means the intense exposure to the sun can burn you in a short time regardless of the season. New Zealand has the highest rate of skin cancer in the world, so sunscreen is a must-have always.

Make sure your passport is valid for at least 3 months before you plan to leave New Zealand. Getting caught out here can cost you hundreds in emergency passport costs plus delays in returning home. Make sure you have a digital copy of your passport and another copy in another place separate from your main passport.

Your driver's license and your international driving permit. If you want to drive in New Zealand, these must be current, not disqualified in your country of origin or in New Zealand. These must be done in English.

Prescription medication, make sure you have enough supply for the duration of your trip. You can bring up to 3 months' supply of prescription medication at a time through customs. Any more than that needs to be covered by a letter from your doctor.

Ensure you have your visa and all paperwork finalised before you leave on your trip. It is important to state that it is your responsibility to make sure you have the correct visas and paperwork.

Your swimwear is essential whether it is for swimming or relaxing in one of the country's hot pools. If it is summer, you can swim daily in the sea or local pools or pools at your accommodation. Or partake in water sports.

5-7 pairs of underwear and the same for socks

1 set of casual clothing for going out.

1 set of good clothes for going out for fancy dinners or a live show.

2-3 tank tops or tee shirts

3 pairs of pants or skirts

1 hat & a light scarf

Sunglasses

Water-resistant watch

What Not to Pack

Sports gear or scuba gear as these can be hired. The same with skis and surfboards.

Books, except for maybe one for the flight there and back.

An outfit for every day. You won't need this level of clothing.

Loads of toiletries or make-up

Hair styling tools and products

More than two devices

Expensive accessories, like watches and jewelry.

Sheets and heavy towels

Uncomfortable and impractical footwear

Just in case gear, like umbrellas

Digital Pack List

Digital Camera and Camera Bag

Mini HD video camera

I-Pod Music Player

Laptop

Tablet/Kindle

Electronic Chargers and adapter

Pack light, coming to New Zealand. This way, there will be space to bring back all the treasures and souvenirs you just had to get. If you reach the limits of your luggage weight allowance going home, great, no extra charge. If you go over by a couple of kilos, you won't be pinged for a huge bill.

Typical Food & Drink of New Zealand

Kiwis love their food, and they love sharing the spoils with visitors. While you are here, seek out a few of the local delicacies.

Number one on the list is crayfish and seafood. Being surrounded by stunning coastline from North to South means seafood is plentiful, and New Zealand seafood enjoys a reputation of being the best in the world. You can try Green lip muscles, King salmon, crayfish or scallops and oysters.

Succulent and tender lamb roast is a Kiwi favourite and is one of the country's top export meats. Best enjoyed with seasonal roast vegetables and greens, you will find it on menus in many local restaurants.

Hangi is the traditional earth oven way of cooking. The food steams underground for several hours. Hangi is often served as celebration food. Foods cooked in a Hangi include chicken, pork, and mutton, as well as potatoes, pumpkin and kumara (sweet potato). You may also be served Hangi Steam pudding for dessert. If you visit Rotorua, you will be able to experience this cultural dish.

Fish and chips are best enjoyed sitting on a beach on a warm evening. The sea gulls can get a bit noisy for their share of the food. They are not the type of bird to come and snatch the food, though, unless you leave it unattended. You can find them in almost every town and city in New Zealand, and they are delicious with white bread and tomato sauce.

New Zealand beer and wine are enjoyed all over the world. A full-bodied pinot or a fresh and fruity Sauvignon Blanc. Found on restaurant menus everywhere, this is your chance to enjoy these New Zealand flavours. Craft beer is enjoying a rise in popularity too. Since 1907 in Paeroa, a soft drink named Lemon & Paeroa (L&P) has enjoyed a reputation all over New Zealand and can be found in supermarkets and dairies all over the country. The name stems from being created in the town of Paeroa. Other drinks include Feijoa juices or smoothies, natural kiwifruit, apple juices or healthy kombuchas. Found locally everywhere.

The Kiwi summer BBQ is cooking outdoors on a gas or wood-run BBQ. The BBQ is an essential part of Kiwi culture and has moved on from sausages and chops. You can cook lamb, beef, and chicken. Usually served alongside potato salad and lettuce salad. Family and friends come together to enjoy the meal outside.

Kiwis love their Hokey Pokey ice cream, and this is a must-try for tourists. Creamy vanilla ice cream with little balls of honeycomb. More so served with Pavlova, a meringue-based dessert topped with fresh whipped cream and fruit. A Christmas table in New Zealand is not often without a Pavlova.

New Zealand chocolate and lollies are another favourite. Whitakers' chocolate is at the top of the favourite list, followed closely by Cookie Time Cookies. There is a range of flavours both in the chocolate and cookie creations. Kiwis also enjoy pineapple lumps and

Jaffa's, quintessential New Zealand lollies.

New Zealand pies now have a range of flavours, limited only by the baker's imagination. Always encrusted in a flaky pastry and served in a brown paper bag. Try flavours such as Hangi pie or creamed paua pie. New Zealand pies are award-winning.

New Zealand cheese is a delicacy you cannot afford to turn up. New Zealand boasts world-class cheese makers. Made not only from cow's milk but sheep and goats milk too. Famous for blue cheeses, sharp vintages, or soft creamy cheeses. Kapiti cheeses, Whitestone and Puhoi Valley are New Zealand's favourites.

There are two major players in the New Zealand supermarket scene. Pak'n'Save and Countdown. Pak'n'Save is New Zealand owned and operated and marginally cheaper, while Countdown is Australian-owned. Under the Pak'n'Save umbrella are New World, Four Square, Gilmores and Liquor land.

Every region has all the major players plus Asian food stores and independent fruit and vegetable outlets.

Transport Options

Hire a Campervan

From $29.00 a day plus fuel and bond and insurance, you can carry your accommodation around on wheels. You need a clean driver's licence and to study the NZ Road Code to know how to drive on New Zealand roads. You need to know the workings of your campervan, such as where to dispose of grey water and where to fill the freshwater tank. Campgrounds have these facilities or know where they are located. This type of accommodation can keep you independent or give you a degree of privacy. However, it can get expensive very quickly.

Modes of Public Transport

Most regions have their own local bus service or train service. Christchurch has trams and local buses. While Auckland also has local ferry services from the city to the North Shore of Auckland, which would take about 2 hours by bus. Buses and trains service most areas in Auckland.

The ferry takes 40 minutes. Every region has its own Taxi service, and Taxis are available 24/7. These can get expensive, so you may not want to have your transport budget swallowed whole by Taxis, but they are good for getting back to your accommodation late at night or getting somewhere in a hurry.

Uber is another great invention, costing half the price of a Taxi. In each region, you download the Uber App on your phone and then book an Uber when you need one, and they pick you up when you are ready. They usually take up to 3 minutes to arrive and are efficient at getting you from point to point quickly.

Air NZ is our national airline carrier. They service most regions. You can get great deals from Grab a Seat on their website. They often advertise on social media and deal between main centres for less than $120.00 one way for a seat only.

Rental cars are another option for transport. Hiring costs include a security deposit, a daily hiring rate of between $14 and $73.00 per day, plus the costs of fueling the car as you go on your road trip. This can work out cheaper if it's for a few days but watch out for those parking costs too. You will be able to drive in New Zealand on your overseas drivers' for 12 months from the last date of entry into New Zealand. Your license must be current and not disqualified in the country it was issued, and your license must not have been suspended in New Zealand.

Your car rental company will be able to advise you further as per conditions and if you are eligible to drive in New Zealand on an overseas license.

Here in New Zealand, we drive on the left-hand side of the road, which may be different from your country of origin. All drivers must know New Zealand road rules, what the road signs mean and how to drive safely. You can find out more in The official New Zealand Road Code.

The best transport option for travel around New

Zealand by far is the Intercity Bus Flexi-Pass. It's an hours-based travel pass that allows you to plan your own itinerary and travel. The bus passes can be managed online, topped up to extend the hours if exploring takes longer, bus booked anywhere for any time. These range in price from 10 hours at $98.00 to 80 hours at $561.00. Flexi- bus travel also allows you to catch the Interisland ferry and the Trans-Alpine Train. Flexi-Passes are valid for 12 months.

Play, Stay, Do & See

The following itinerary example will consume a 60-hour Flexi-Bus Pass. More hours can be added for any unforeseen extras. The cost is $472.00.

Auckland is where you will land in the country and so it makes sense to start from this point. I am going to show you, how to see New Zealand from Cape Reinga to Stewart Island in 35 days.

The most cost-effective way to do this trip is to purchase a 60-hour flexi-bus pass from Intercity at a cost of $472.00. The pass will get you onto the ferry to cross the Cook Straight and travel on the Trans Alpine Train to Christchurch for no extra cost.

The weather in Auckland in the Summer is hot and sticky with the temperature up around 28-30 degrees. In the Winter Auckland sees a lot of rain with a temperature drop to 12-15 degrees. High winds can also buffet the city of sails.

Day 1 & 2: Auckland

Auckland is New Zealand's largest city. The city is situated between two harbours and dotted with 48 extinct volcanos. In Auckland you can enjoy marine adventures, wine trails, forest walks and urban sophistication.

Board a ferry at Auckland Ferry Terminal and head over to Waiheke Island, known as the 'island of wine'. In landscape and lifestyle Waiheke is a world away from Downtown Auckland.

If you are a walker, explore one of Waiheke's trails along clifftops, down into beaches or into the coolness of the forest.

Staying overnight on Waiheke is easy, rent out a beach

house or for the budget option stay at one of the friendly backpackers on offer.

Enjoy the art and culture by visiting the Auckland War Memorial Museum and the Auckland Art Gallery. Indulge in the shopping and restaurant scene.

Relax with Glamping under the stars. Enjoy activities like clay shooting, archery, and much more. Epic sea views, gourmet meals, luxury spa and beauty treatments await you with this glamping experience.

Check out the local food scene with Matakana market. Home of beautiful beaches, local art, local vineyards make this village a go to destination. Pick up organic, seasonal produce or savor some fresh delicacies by the river's edge.

Auckland is known for its diverse food range, so there is something for everyone. Auckland sports some world class food producers making dining a real gastronomic experience.

For the adrenaline junkies, there is something for you too.

How about a sky walk 192 metres above the ground

along the edge of Auckland's sky tower, the tallest building in New Zealand. Or if your nerves can handle it, a sky jump off the same building.

Kayak to Rangitoto Island at sunset to take in the night sky, bush walks and a BBQ dinner and refreshments.

Then there is the Auckland Harbour bridge climb or a chance to bungy jump off the same structure.

On Waiheke Island take part in the Eco Zip Flying Fox adventure or the Waiheke Dive and Snorkel for underwater sights.

HIT Hostel is a popular choice among backpackers or the Fort Street Accommodation is another go to choice. Glamping for a touch of luxury will put a spring in your step for the rest of your trip.

The city of sails lights up at night with the Sky City Casino right in the city centre. This is a huge complex with a hotel, restaurants and two casino floors. The star of the restaurant show is Orbit 360 at the top of Sky Tower featuring a rotating dining room with panoramic windows. The dining room rotates once every hour, providing 360-degree views of the city, the Hauraki Gulf and more.

Orbit offers a modern dining experience with a delicious kiwi inspired a la catre menu. Orbit is New Zealand's only rotating restaurant so take the opportunity while you are in Auckland to sample this unique experience.

From Broadway to ballet, film festivals, pick from a plethora of shows at one of the city centre's state of the art performing arts theatres. The Grand old Lady of Theatres, the Civic is the iconic art deco building that hosts many international shows.

The ASB Waterfront Theatre, home of the Auckland Theatre Company hots both domestic and international arts organisations to tour. The theatre has a café on site, Halsey St Kitchen open from Monday to Friday during the show season for dinning two hours prior to every performance.

The Herald Theatre hosts everything from new theatre by top local artists and international playwrights to international micro-circuses.

Sky City has its own 700 seat theatre with state-of-the-art staging and cinema features which are perfect for international and local events.

Other theatres or theatrettes grace the city, the ones mentioned above are where all the main shows run.

Price List for Accommodation & Main Activities

Ferry Tickets to and from Waiheke - $42.00 Adult

Return Deal - $35.00 Adult

Hop-On Hop-Off - $68.00 Adult

Accommodation Waiheke - From: $33.00 per night Adult

HIT Hostel Auckland - From: $52.00 per night Adult

Fort St Backpackers Auckland - From: $41.00 per night Adult

Glamping Holiday Splurge - $380-430.00 per night

Eco Zip Adventures Waiheke - From: $129.00

Waiheke Dive & Snorkel - From: $69.00

Sky Jump off the Sky Tower - $255.00

Sky Walk - $150.00

Evening Kayak to Rangitoto Island - $163.00 pp BBQ Dinner & Refreshments

Auckland Harbour Bridge Climb - $130.00

Auckland Harbour Bridge Bungy - $165.00

Auckland Whale & Dolphin Safari - From: $129.00

Orbit 360 Dining - $89.00 pp for 3 Courses

Day 3 -6: Bay of Islands & Cape Reinga

Using your Flexi-Bus Pass for the first time, travel 4 hours and 10 minutes to the town of Paihia, which makes an excellent base for exploration and fun in the Bay of islands. You can do so much in three days, so here goes, Cruises of all types leave the wharf each day. If Water sports is your thing you have come to the right place.

Arrange a trip to the outer islands and hook into a fishing expedition

Catch the Ferry to Russell for the day

Learn the beginnings of our nation with a visit to the historic Treaty House at the Treaty of Waitangi Grounds.

Visit the Whangarei Falls, where you will find an impressive waterfall and a boardwalk.

Do a day trip to Cape Reinga and 90-mile Beach

Discover the Waipoua Forest

Enjoy a drink at the Duke of Marlborough in Russell which holds New Zealand's first liquor license.

For the more fit and active traveller:

Cycle from Coast to Coast

Sandboarding down some of the largest sand dunes in the Southern Hemisphere

Off-road driving on 90-mile Beach

Ocean Adventure – the fastest boat to the Hole in the Rock

Bay of Islands Parasail

Mountain Bike Hire to take on the trails round Paihia

The YHA is a popular choice in Paihia, although for backpackers' accommodation in the Bay of Islands you will be spoilt for choice, there are so many. Make a base at the Base, bay of Islands or try the Saltwater Lodge. The Top 10 Holiday Park is great if you have a young family in tow. Haka Lodge in Paihia is another great choice.

Enjoy a relaxing 2-and-a-half-hour dinner cruise up the Waitangi River. Billed as 'The Bay's Best Night Out!' you can sit back and marvel in the tranquil surroundings as you take a journey rich with birdlife and historical points of interest. Darryl's Dinner Cruise chef has had 20plus years' experience. The friendly crew on board will cater to all your dinning needs.

The Bay of Islands is also famous for their Twilight and Night Kayak Safari. Cruise and explore the mangrove forest then slide up the Waitangi River to take in the Haruru Falls.

There are a number of Bars and Clubs to finish your night off after dinner, try the Sandpit Poolroom and Bar or the Pipi patch Bar or the Saltwater Bar for drinks and music.

Price List for Accommodation & Main Activities

Fishing Trips From: $270.00 Adult

Darryl's Dinner Cruise $109.00 pp Adult

Cape Reinga & 90-mile beach $165.00pp Adult

Waitangi Treaty Grounds Pass $25-50pp Adult

The fastest Boat to the Hole From $135.00pp Adult

Bay of Islands Parasail $95-135.00pp Adult

Mountain Bike Hire $59-220.00 pp

Haka Lodge $29-89.00 pn

YHA $25-132.00 pn

Top 10 Holiday Park $20-180.00 pn

Saltwater Lodge $25-170.00 pn

Base Bay of Islands $26-85 pn

Day 7 – 10: Coromandel & Rotorua

Catching the bus back to Auckland and transferring there is the best way to get to Coromandel via public transport. The trip takes 4 hours, including a transfer at Thames. Coromandel is a resort town for tourists and locals alike. You can also catch a ferry to the Coromandel, a 2-hour trip, but this will cost extra.

It was formally a Goldmining and timber region and is now home to artists, craftspeople, and conservation preservers. Coromandel has a Victorian theme with many of the Victorian buildings restored.

Coromandel makes a great base for exploring walking tracks, beaches, and, of course, the driving creek train through the Kauri forest where you can check out the local potters' and their wares, or even take a pottery class.

The Driving Creek Train runs on New Zealand's only narrow-gauge mountain railway journey. Pottery sculptures and tile murals line the track and when you arrive the top, spectacular views over the Hauraki Gulf, await you. Climb the 'Eye full' Tower to take photos and don't forget to purchase the local pottery.

Soak in Geothermal Waters of The Lost Spring Day Spa & Dinning.

Hike the Pinnacles, stay overnight in a DOC (Department of Conservation) Hut and reach the summit in the morning for the sun rise.

Cathedral Cove & Hot water Express Tour

Dig your own hot pool at Hot water beach

Learn about the ancient history of goldmining.

For the adrenaline junkies:

Coromandel Zipline Tours.

Cathedral Cove Dive & Snorkel

Cathedral Cove Kayak

Sea Cave Adventures Tour

Visit the Owharoa Falls in Karangahake Gorge -cycle the Haruki Rail Track

Walk the Coromandel Coast

The Top 10 Holiday Park is great for families and backpackers alike. On Hot water beach. Opoutere Coast Camping offers self-contained cabin and caravans as well as tent sites. Anna's Whare and Cottages for that homely feel. River glen Camp offers the same set up as similar camping facilities in the area. If you are big on fishing, then the Anglers Lodge Motel and Holiday Park is for you. Anchor Lodge Backpackers is great value for money and comfort.

There is a wide range of bars and clubs to choose from in the Coromandel for fine dining and an evening of dancing, playing pool or listening to the local D.J's strut their stuff. Cuisine from the mirid of restaurants ranges from Irish, Singaporean, Steak house/casual dining and fine dining al la carte.

Price List for Accommodation & Main Activities

Driving Creek Railway $32-35 Adult

Coromandel Zipline Tours From $127.00 Adult

The Lost Spring Whitianga $49.00 – 900.00 Adult

Cathedral Cove Dive and Snorkel $25.00 – 250.00 Adult

Cathedral Cove Kayak Tours $125.00 – 205.00 Adult

Sea Cave Adventures Tour $70.00-95.00 Adult

Cathedral Cove & Hot Water Express From $115.00 Adult

Hot Water Beach Top 10 $20.00 – 295.00 pn

Opoutere Coast Camping $15 – 200.00 pn

Anna's Whare & Cottages $45.00 – 75.00 pn

River Glen Camp $10.00 – 120.00 pn

Anglers Lodge & Motel $18.00 – 230.00 pn

Anchor Lodge Backpackers $23.00 – 65.00 pn

Rotorua

From the Coromandel catch the bus back to Auckland so you can start your trip to Rotorua in style. To start your trip to Rotorua, indulge in the Hobbiton Afternoon Tour. You get door to door pick up and return to either Auckland or Rotorua.

Enjoy a scenic drive with informative drivers. The tour also includes admission to the guided tour at the Hobbiton Movie Set with a complementary drink at the Green Dragon. Lunch is not included in this deal; however, you can get lunch from the Shires Rest café.

You arrive at your accommodation in Rotorua, saving hours on your flexi-pass, via Flexi-Tours NZ. Rotorua is well-known around the world for its geothermal activity, Māori culture, hot springs, and mud pools.

Experience the hospitality of the people and a fully immersive experience, capture the sights, food, and sounds at Tamaki Māori Village. Voted as the 7th best attraction in the world by Trip Advisor.

Tamaki Māori Village shapes your cultural view of

New Zealand. It is situated 15kms south of Rotorua surrounded by a 200-year-old native Tawa forest. The Highlight of this experience is the Tamaki Māori Village Evening Experience.

Visitors are invited to participate in learning the Poi and the Haka and enjoy dance performances. There is return transportation from and to your accommodation. You will be welcomed in a traditional ceremony and for 3.5 immersed into an interactive tour of a pre-European village.

Then you will be treated to a traditional dinner and dessert feast. Beginning with forest canapes and a complimentary chef choice aperitif before going onto the 4-course feast. This is shared against a backdrop of blazing bonfires and the native forest surrounds.

Local shopping and Cafes

Indulge in a therapeutic hot pool or mud bath

Craft Fairs

For the fit, young, and able:

Head to Velocity Valley for a day jam packed with fun. Ride a BMX bike into a huge airbag. Try the reverse bungy or swoop from 40 metres in the air.

Explore Waimangu Volcanic Valley Geothermal Wonderland.

Raft down a seven-metre-high waterfall.

Zipline through a 119-year-old forest.

Redwoods Nightlights Tree walk.

Mountain bike the Whakarewarewa Forest.

Experience the ZORB, turn yourself into a human bubble

There are accommodation options galore in Rotorua with the Base Hostel hitting the high notes with two mineral pools and a heated outdoor swimming pool as well as the usual hostel amenities.

There is a number of Holiday Park accommodations, including Rotorua Thermal, Blue Lake Top 10, Rotorua Top 10, and Holden's Bay Holiday Park. Rock Solid

Backpackers voted number 1 by Trip Advisor is an excellent option.

Aforementioned is a number of evening activities you can partake in. There are also Movies, Clubs and bars offering dancing, quiet drinks, local and international D.Js, and Pool Rooms.

Price List for Accommodation & Main Activities

Hobbiton Afternoon Tour $189.00 Adult

Tamaki Māori Village $245.00 Adult

Waimangu Volcanic Valley $44.00 - 245.00 Adult

Velocity Valley $55.00 – 289.00 Adult

Rafting Down a Waterfall $109.00 – 164.00 Adult

Ziplining Ultimate Canopy Tour $199.00

Redwoods Nightlights $35.00

Mountain Bike Rotorua $25.00 - 130.00

Polynesian Spa $22.95 - 300.00

ZORB Rotorua $45.00 -160.00

Base Rotorua $26.00 - 70.00 pn

Rotorua Thermal Holiday Park $25.00 – 3000.00pn

Rock Solid Backpackers Hostel $23.00 - 95.00pn

Blue Lake Top 10 Holiday Park $40.00 – 289.00pn

Rotorua Top 10 Holiday Park $27.00 – 300.00pn

Holdens Bay Holiday Park $20.00 – 180.00pn

Day 11-13:Taupo & Napier

One hour from Rotorua is Taupo is centrally located in the middle of the North Island. Taupo has some of the North Island's most impressive scenery and the Taupo is perfect for all you adrenaline junkies with outdoor activities galore.

Walking and hiking, water skiing, sailing, and fishing. Snow skiing in the Winter on Mt Ruapehu. For the more sedate travellers, Taupo is home to a range of naturally heated hot pools.

Taupo has something for everyone, local markets and cafes and souvenir shopping. Indulge in thermal pools and fine dining.

Encounter geothermal wonderlands. The Valley of Orakei Korako Cave and Thermal Park. Accessible only by ferry across Lake Ohakuri.

Indulge your sweet tooth at Huka Honey Hive, sample delicious New Zealand Honey which is famous for its purity and healing properties. Take a tour that teaches you about the benefits of Manuka honey, royal jelly, and bee pollen. Enjoy a honey ice cream during your visit.

Soak in geothermal waters at Wairakei Terraces. Soak in naturally heated geothermal pools below ancient silica terraces.

Take a guided hike on the Tongariro Crossing, New Zealand's greatest day walk.

Enjoy a cocktail evening aboard the Ernest Kemp Cocktail Cruise to the Māori Rock Carvings.

Go to the popular with the locals, Taupo Debrett's Hot Springs for a soak or a swim.

Sail Barbury Eco Sailing on Lake Taupo.

Visit the Huka Falls, one of new Zealand's most popular attractions.

Huka Falls River Cruise

Huka Prawn Park

Holiday Splurge at the Edgewater Millennium Restaurant with award winning food and wine.

Boutique Shopping at Taupo Town Centre

For the athletic among us:

Huka Falls Jet Boat

Taupo Bungy

Taupo Swing

Wairakei Terraces

Tongariro Alpine Crossing

Jet Ski Hire on lake Taupo

Confinement Escape Rooms Taupo

Taupo Lake Adventures Ltd Trout Fishing Charters

Taupo is a hot tourist spot; accommodation is plentiful and priced for backpackers. There is luxury accommodation in Taupo if you have allowed for a luxury accommodation splurge during your holiday or you can save it until the end of your trip. There is the YHA Taupo, the Base Backpackers, Huka Lodge Taupo, Based by the Lake Accommodation and Taupo Urban Retreat to name but a few.

Enjoy an evening cruise on the lake or you can kayak at sunset on Lake Taupo. Sample the local food culture. If you are looking for something a bit more robust, do some night fishing. You can Party lake Taupo style with the Element Bar or Urban retreat, both backpackers' bars. There are loads of bars and clubs to choose and let your hair down.

Stargaze at the Southern Hemisphere sky, even with the lights on in town, on a clear night there is still an impressive display of stars. You can try from some of the camp sites around the lake for an uninterrupted view of the night skies. You can take in a good movie at the cinema or if it's Friday check out the Night Food Market.

Price List for Accommodation & Main Activities

Taupo lake Adventures Ltd Trout Fishing Charters $160 – 340.00 Adult

Sunset Kayaking $35.00 per hour Adult

Orakei Korako Cave & Thermal Park $42.00 Adult

Huka Honey Hive

Wairakei Terraces $25.00 Adult

Adrift Tongariro Alpine Crossing $195 – 325.00 Adult

Ernest Kemp Cocktail Cruise to the Māori Rock Carvings

Confinement Escape Rooms $35.00 Adult

Catch the Huka Falls Bus $4.00 Adult

Taupo Debretts Hot Springs $11.00 – 25.00 Adult

Sail Barbury Eco Sailing – Lake Taupo $49.00 – 59.00

Adult

    Huka Falls River Cruise From $42.00 Adult

    Taupo Bungy From $185.00 Adult

    Taupo Swing From $160.00 Adult

    Huka Prawn Park From $25.00 Adult

    Edgewater Restaurant (Holiday Splurge) From $90.00 for 3 Courses

    LakeFun Jet Ski Hire $120.00

    YHA Taupo $23.00 – 120.00 pn

    Base Backpackers $90.00 pn

    Huka Lodge Taupo $47.00 pn

    Based by the Lake Accommodation $70.00 pn

    Taupo Urban Retreat From $22.00 pn

Napier

Travelling from Taupo to Napier is a 12-hour overnight trip, leaving at 5.30pm, so you will save on accommodation for the night. Beautifully preserved 1930's architecture is what makes Napier unique. No other city in New Zealand has these special features in their buildings. It is an art connoisseur's mecca. Souvenir shops, shopping, art galleries and Dolphin world to name a few of the attractions on offer in Napier. A huge earthquake in 1931 rocked Hawkes Bay for more than three minutes, killing close to 260 people and levelling the city centre.

Rebuilding begun and new buildings were created in the art deco style of the times – Stripped, Classical, Spanish Mission and Art Deco. Enjoy the streets by exploring on foot – ask for a map at the information centre or at the Art Deco Trust.

Talk a walk back in time with a guided walking tour. Your guide will tell you the stories of the earthquake that destroyed the city and the rebuild and recovery completed in less than two years.

Sea Wall murals are dotted around the city covering up to 50 walls. Take a map and walk or bus around the city to see them up close.

Church Road Winery sampling the latest range while being guided through a blind tasting.

Art deco Centre for gifts, books, and keepsakes.

The National Aquarium of New Zealand where you can discover an exciting world both under and above the water. See Penguin Cove and watch the Penguins as they go about their daily lives. See huge stingrays and sharks swimming over you in the 1.5 million litre oceanarium.

Napier City Bike Hire & Tours, hire a bike and take in the tracks around Napier.

Par2 Mini Golf opposite Napier's I-Site Visitor Centre. 18 Hole putting courses are perfect for challenging others to a game.

Laser force, live action laser tag game experience with state-of-the-art electronic equipment.

Visit the Silky Oak Chocolate Company Ltd, taste,

smell and learn all about chocolate at the factory/shop, museum, Pantry, and café. Don't forget to ask about the Triple Layer Dipper.

If you are a thrill seeker and not faint of heart, try Mohaka Rafting, choose from Grade 3, 4 or 5.

Laser force tag live game experience with the latest electronic equipment

Super trike to view scenic Te Mata Peak

Surfing

The Art House will suit beach goers and shoppers alike being close to town and 1 minute walk from the beach. Wally's is another great stay in backpackers accommodation. Along with all the standard facilities, Wally's has an Outdoor area with free gas BBQs. Great for socialising with a few drinks.

Dotted around the city within walking distance of town is Archie's Bunker, Stables Lodge is 5 minutes' walk to the city, close to all bus depots and 50 m to the ocean. The Criterion Art Deco Backpackers is right in the heart of the city, house in a Spanish Mission style building.

Live entertainment is at the Napier Party Bars Nightclub and Monica Loves. The Rose Irish Pub has great food, and the Guinness is flowing, great for watching live sport and bar games. They have quiz nights and live music.

If you fancy yourself a rockstar have a go at Karaoke at The Wind Sports bar. Have an explore of the inner city to check out the food culture among the clubs and Bars and enjoy your night. Catch one of the many concerts advertised weekly at backpackers and the I-Site.

Price List for Accommodation & Main Activities

Art Deco Guided Walks $28.00 – 30.00 Adult

Sea Wall Murals – Self Guided walks Free

Church Road Winery From $35.00 Adult

Aquarium $17.50 – 24.00 Adult

Napier City Bike Hire & Tours $20.00 – 85.00

Par2 Mini Golf From $10.90

Mohaka Rafting – Grade 3 Rafting From $175.00

Laser Force $9.00 -11.00

The Silky Oak Chocolate Company Ltd $8.00 – 84.00

Super Trike Te Mata Peak From $169.00

The Art House Backpackers From $25.00 pn

Wally's Backpackers From $23.00 – 60.00 pn

Archie's Bunker Backpackers From $27.00 pn

Stables Lodge Backpackers From $27.29 pn

Day 14 & 17: Wellington & Wairarapa

Jumping back on the bus in Napier, wander South 7.5 hours down the classic wine trail to Wellington. There is a lot to squeeze into a couple of days in this region. Arriving around 4.00pm in the afternoon. You might like to head to your accommodation, unpack and freshen up before finding a bite to eat and some night life.

Dubbed 'the coolest little capital in the world' by Lonely

Planet, Wellington offers a powerful blast of history, nature, culture, and cuisine. Fueled by strong coffee and world-class craft beer, you will be ready for action.

Home of Peter Jackson's Lord of The Rings Movies

Speaking of action Wellington is the home of Peter Jackson's Lord of the Rings. Dual companies Weta workshop and Weta digital are responsible for the world renown films and other blockbusters which include The Hobbit, King Kong, The Avengers and Ghost in the Shell. TV series include District 9 James Cameron of 'Titanic' fame came here to film the Oscar winning movie, Avatar because he was determined to make a ground-breaking movie.

So, if you are a film buff these tours are for you. Weta Studio Tours, explore 20 years of creativity and film making. Learn about making movie effects and props, armour, weapons, creatures and costumes, make-up, and miniatures.

The tour takes two hours and Weta's store where you can buy anything movie is a sight to behold. It is full of collectables, books, swords, and games and lots more. The Museum attached is free. It is strongly recommended you book in advance online because tickets for the tour sell out fast, especially during the peak season from Oct-April.

The Embassy theatre built in 1926 hosted the film premier of The Hobbit: An unexpected Journey. View the nameplates of the characters and actors names, situated by the leather seats.

Roxy theatre is owned by the co-founders of the Weta Workshop and features the art deco period blended with modern 21st century movie technology. Enjoy a meal at the CoCo restaurant, feast on local food. View the stunning Weta Workshop artwork dotted through-out the building.

The first day of shooting for The Lord of the Rings Trilogy was filmed on Mt Victoria on the town belt. The Hobbiton Woods was also filmed here. Mt Victoria has views across Wellington City and the harbour.

On the waterfront you will find New Zealand's National Museum (Te Papa) held up as one of the best interactive museums in the world. Take in a guided tour with the knowledgeable and friendly Te Papa Hosts. The guided tours add a depth to the experience of New Zealand's rich history by making it come alive for you. The tour takes 60 minutes and departs 3 times a day.

Visit Hannah's Laneway for eclectic shopping, cafes, and bars.

Ride the Wellington Cable Car up to the look out for panoramic views over the city. Nearby is the Cable Car Museum and the Botanic Gardens.

Stargazers can observe the night skies from Carter Observatory's telescope, catch a Planetarium show or see the interactive museum.

Spend the day or half a day up close and personal with New Zealand's native birds and a prehistoric reptile.

Attend a Wellington Event, with St James theatre and the opera house both in Courtney Place, you can attend concerts, live theatre. Other festivals include The World of Wearable Arts, visual arts combining lights and fashion. Try catching a live sporting event at the Westpac Stadium up the ramp coming from the railway station.

Know as New Zealand's culinary capital, you won't struggle to find tastes that dance across your taste buds in Wellington. Try Logan Brown, Manners St Deli, Pie and Pickle to name 3 of the range of choices.

Makara peak Mountain bike Park has enough tracks to please everyone, from intermediate to expert grade. Every metre of the track has been hand built by bike enthusiasts over 15 years. Hire your bike from Mud Cycles Kaori and head out to have fun.

Windsurfing or Kitesurfing on Wellington Harbour or try Cook Strait. Hire boards at Real Surf, Lyall Bay, Wellington.

Wellington Fear Factory Haunted House.

Bucking Bronco at Valhalla on Vivian Street.

You will find pub crawls, karaoke nights and pool tournaments in Wellington Backpackers because the emphasis is on socialising. All the following Backpackers are close to the action of the city. Hotel Waterloo & Backpackers, Nomads Capital Hostel within a 15-minute walk to Courtney Place. Trek Global is close to town and parks. The following hostels are in the CBD, The Marion Hotel, and the Dwellington, and the Cambridge Hotel.

Wellington has one of the vibist atmospheres that

comes out after dark. Party central is Courtney Place with a wide range of pubs, clubs, and restaurants. Danger Danger is one such place blasting out 80's and 90's beats long into the early hours of the morning. Dance the night away. Night Club Public can be relied upon to keep your dancing the night away.

For something a bit different Valhalla on Vivian Street house, a Bucking bronco. Grab your cowboy hat and see how long you can ride the bucking bull.

Wellington has a live calendar of events all year round. The home of live shows is the TSB Arena on Queens Wharf which is the largest indoor venue in the city. The Michael Fowler Centre host the New Zealand Symphony Orchestra and the Centre is an iconic landmark in Wellington.

Catch a show in dance, drama, opera, comedy, and cabaret at iconic Wellington Theatre, St James. Known as The Jimmy to the locals.

Want to laugh your head off? The Fringe Comedy Club is the place to tickle your ribs with stand up comedy both local and international. The Caravan Club often hosts live comedy and rock and roll evenings, all those tunes from a bygone era.

A premium movie theatre in Courtney Place means you can catch a movie in state-of-the-art theatres. If you want luxury, and comfort with a footrest, wine and food during your movie buy the gold class ticket.

Price List for Accommodation & Main Activities

Weta Studios Tour $49.00 Adult

Guided Tour of Te Papa $20.00 Adult

Wellington Cable Car $9.00 Adult

Space Place Carter Observatory $14.00 Adult

Zealandia $23.00 Adult

Makara Peak Mountain Bike Park $40 -60.00 hire for 2 hours from Mud Cycles

Windsurfing or Kitesurfing From Real Surf $60.00 for 2-hour hire

Wellington Fear Factory Haunted House From $35.00 pp

Hotel Waterloo & Backpackers From $29.00 pn

Nomads Capital Hostel From $23.00 pn

The Marion Hostel From $34.00 pn

Trek Global Backpackers From $28.00 pn

The Dwellington From $35.75 pn

The Cambridge Hotel & Backpackers From $35.00 pn

Martinborough

If you land in Martinborough, Wairarapa at the end of November you are in for a treat.

Martinborough is located an hour out of Wellington by train. There is a daily service of 4 trains. Take the train to Featherston station then transfer to bus line 200 for an 18-minute trip to Martinborough. Another option is to book a shuttle via Rimutaka Shuttles or Carterton Shuttles.

Martinborough began in 1870 as a place called Wharekaka. In the first 10 years, churches, a school, a hotel and general store and Post office opened. In 1879, John Martin, who was an Irish immigrant and a wealthy landowner purchased land and founded a new town naming it after himself.

Martinborough is a modern compact and accessible wine village. The wineries are all located close together for ease of walking or biking between each one. This little village is famous not just for its wineries but for its yearly festival, Toast Martinborough.

The Toast Martinborough festival date has been moved to Sunday 20th November 2022, this year. This is the most talked about and sought-after festival from near and far. It is a unique one-day event which sports multiple site events and the vineyards offering wonderful wine and food and music choices through the day.

This premium event first started in 1992 and has shown the heart of a unique wine village. It is a true celebration for lovers of fine wine, gourmet food and talented musicians.

At this festival of the year the organisers want you to have the best day ever. So, they recommend you plan your day in advance, like how you are getting to and home from the event. The day begins at 8.00am in The Martinborough Square in the heart of the township.

This is where you exchange your ticket for a wristband, a shatter-proof toast Martinborough glass and lanyard. The day ends at 4.00pm. Participating sites are open from 10.00am until 6.00pm with all wine sales finishing at 5.00pm.

If you are traveling by charter bus, or by car, there is free parking at the Martinborough Rugby grounds for free. There is a coffee cart, a bank and toilet facilities at the Rugby grounds too.

Purchasing food and drinks is a cashless process which means there is no need to que up at the bank. Payment methods accepted at PayWave EFTPOS or PayWave CREDITCARD. The good news about this change is you can top up your wristband and you will not have to worry about a refund at the end of the event.

At the beginning of the day, you will receive a wristband, and this wristband will allow you into each site by scanning in. With the loaded funds on your wristband, you will be able to make your purchases of food and wine.

There is a dress to impress competition with roving judges giving out spot prizes to the classiest girls and guys. Top prize for the day? The insta-fame, plus a double pass for Toast in November 2023 and a gift pack to celebrate in style at home or with a return trip to Martinborough.

There is an array of merchandise and posters available for purchase to commemorate the event. These are available at all the event sites. So be sure to pick up a memento of the best day ever.

On your last night wind down your day with glass of local wine and a meal at one of the many cafes on Courtney Place. Turn in for the night because tomorrow you are catching the ferry to Picton in the South Island.

South Island

By now you will realise what a valuable travel asset the Intercity Travel pass has been for you. It's about to get better, because you can travel on the ferry, trains & buses. Regional local buses and trains are not included in the Travel Pass.

Day 18-20: Marlborough & Kaikoura

This area is famous for sunshine, wine, and the Marlborough Sounds. Blenheim and Picton are great bases to explore this region from.

Picton is the heart of Marlborough Sounds. This little port town has cafes, restaurants and galleries, accommodation, and souvenir shops. If you arrive early in the day, you can catch a Cruise & Lunch at Furneaux Lodge in the Marlborough Sounds for $110.00, remember to make booking for this a few days beforehand.

The ferry trip across the Cook Strait is one of the most scenic in the world. Enjoy sheltered inlets, sandy bays, and the clear waters of the Marlborough Sounds. Hike through the forests or kayak around the headlands.

The way to cram everything in you want to do is to base yourself in Blenheim and do a day trip to Kaikoura. For 2 nights' accommodation base yourself at Blenheim Bridges Holiday Park.

After exploring your immediate surroundings, including Wineries, Restaurants, Award winning gardens and parks and the jewel in Blenheim's crown.

Omaka Aviation Heritage Centre, where you can discover world-renowned WWI and WWII exhibits where the aircraft is bought to life in a theatrical manner featuring Peter Jackson's own rare collection of historical aircraft and memorabilia.

For a day of spectacular coast and wildlife encounters, book a day trip to Kaikoura. Catch a bus from Blenheim and 1.5 hours later

Interests & Activities

Eat Crayfish

Go whale watching by boat or air all year round

Swim with or watch dusky dolphins, a truly unforgettable memory.

Swim with the seals

Take a bird watching tour.

Meet the indigenous people and experience Māori

culture with Cultural Artwork package.

    Adventure Activities

    Kaikoura Peninsula Walkway

    Challenging Mountain Bike climbing tracks

    Llama Trekking

    Off-road Glenstrae 4-wheeler Adventures

    Kayaking with the Whales

    Catch a spot of surfing on the local beaches.

If you are exhausted from a full day's activities in Kaikoura, bed down for the night at Dusky Lodge Kaikoura for a good sleep before embarking on further adventures. Your stay in Blenheim for 1 – 2 nights is Blenheim Bridges Holiday Park. Both properties have all the conveniences of modern backpackers around the country.

    There are restaurants, club, pubs, and bars to let your hair down after a day of wildlife encounters or extreme walking or biking track.

Price List for Accommodation & Main Activities

Blenheim Bridges Holiday Park From $35.00 - $155.00 pn Adult

Dusky Lodge From $28.00 - $110.00 pn Adult

Cruise & Lunch in the Sounds $110.00 Adult

Walkways Free

Omaka Aviation Heritage Centre $39.00 both exhibitions Adult

Dolphin Encounter Watch $110.00 Adult

Half Day Llama Trek $119.00 Adult

Off Road 4-Wheeler $95.00 - $159.00 Adult

Bike Hire Coastal Sports $30.00 4 hours & $40.00 8 hours

Surfboard & Wetsuit Hire $40.00 per day

Day 20 – 21: The West Coast

Jump on another bus from Kaikoura because today you are going to cross Arthur's Pass, a well-used route. Today, it is home to Arthur's Pass national Park and is an awesome place for walking.

First stop on the itinerary is Greymouth. This small town on the West Coast has a history of jade hunting, gold mining and dramatic river floods. Sample the beer at the Monteith's Brewery, one of New Zealand's oldest, and listen to the wild West Coast stories.

Greymouth was once the site of the Māori Pa Mawhera (widespread river mouth), referring to Greymouth's river mouth location. While Greymouth is a small town by New Zealand standards, it is the largest town on the West Coast.

Shantytown tells the story of the town's gold mining history. Shantytown is the local Museum that provides a real sense of what it was like living in New Zealand in the 1900's gold mining era. Visitors participate in and observe our country as it was.

Shantytown is one of the West Coast's leading function, conference and wedding venues and is located 10km south of Greymouth.

Local brewery Monteith's is a new Zealand legend; it runs tours that include a tasting session. Around Greymouth you will find galleries specialising in pounamu (New Zealand Jade.

Greymouth hosts sea fishing, fly fishing and a number of adventure activities. The 2-hour Point Elizabeth Walk passes through a scenic reserve and old gold mining sites. It begins 12km north of Greymouth at Rapahoe beach which is also a popular swimming spot in the Summer.

Shantytown Heritage Park

Cycle Journeys

Monteith's Brewery

West coast Massage Therapy

The National Kiwi Centre

Wild Food & Craft Beer Hokitika Wild foods Festival

held yearly.

Adventure Activities

Caving

West Coast Tree Top Walk & Café

Glacier Rafting

Fox & Frans Josef Glaciers

Cycle the Old Ghost Rd 85km of single-track adventure for a daredevil challenge on a Grade 4 track.

Hokitika Gorge Tour 2 hour Guided Tour

Accommodation

Noah's Ark Backpackers

The Theatre Royal Hotel Kumara

The Old Undertakers

Nightlife in Greymouth

Greymouth's clubs, pubs, and bars are a great experience. They offer the atmosphere to have a few brews on a Saturday night, or a delicious hearty meal any night of the week. Most have television screens so you can catch that all important rugby game or cricket match with friends.

After viewing the might rivers of solid ice of the Frans Josef and Fox Glaciers you will be ready for a beer and a hearty meal. Let Hokitika spoil you and entertain you with its wild food and hospitality. They will have you ready for the next leg of your trip.

Price list for Accommodation & Main Activities

Shantytown Heritage Park From $36.00 - $82.00 Adult

Hokitika Scenic Tours Gorge Tour From $85.00 Adult

Cycle Journeys $20.00 - $600.00 Adult

Westcoast Tree Top Walk $32.00 Adult

Glacier Rafting From $135.00 Adult

Westcoast Massage Therapy $20.00 - $99.00

The National Kiwi Centre $24.00 - $27.00

Noah's Ark Backpackers $29.00 - $180.00pn

The Theatre Royal Hotel $27.00pn

The Old Undertakers $30.00 - $50.00

Day 22 – 24: Queenstown & Wanaka

Enjoy waterfalls and river scenery as you leave the Westcoast and travel over Haast Pass to Wanaka. Enjoy a mix of adventure and tranquility.

It is possible to enjoy this region on a budget. Depending on the activities you want to do. If you want a quieter pace of life stay in Wanaka, this is a mini version of Queenstown, but more laid back. If you are an adrenaline junkie there is not contest, stay in Queenstown. Queenstown has more social life at night for those that enjoy nights out making new friends.

Wanaka has some unique attractions like Puzzling World and the quirky Paradiso Cinema. There is an appealing mix for all tastes in Wanaka. You can't go past Wanaka without stopping and photographing the most photographed Pub in the world. The Cardrona Pub. Stop off for an awesome meal and great southern hospitality. For these next two days you need to make a choice about where you want to stay.

Queenstown is known as the adventure capital of the world and is home to the first and most famous bungy jumps. you can experience the thrill of the bungy jump. Queenstown is exciting and sophisticated and scenic. You can source almost any kind of adventure. You can hire any equipment you need, mountain bikes, hiking Packs, Helmets, Hiking Boots, and Skis.

A visit to Arrowtown to see the gorgeous colours of Autumn in April/May.

> Play a round at the challenging golf course

> Puzzling World at Wanaka

> The Lakes District Museum in Arrowtown

> Catch a Movie at the Paradiso Cinema in Wanaka

> Get amongst Queenstown's Food and Wine Culture

Explore one of the many walking trails

Visit the Jellybean Store for art made out of Jellybeans & Jellybeans to eat

Cruise Across Lake Wakatipu on the TSS Earnslaw

Enjoy shopping & Local Markets

Adventure Activities

Bungy Jumping

Jet Boat the Shot over River

Take the Queenstown Gondola

Queenstown Luge

Hydro Attack – A high speed shark Ride – A World First feature

One of the best ways to experience Queenstown is through your tastebuds. Your tastebuds will tell your heart a story, leading with the dance as flavours tango across your palate.

Try a Fergburger, these are famous among the locals. Look out for their merchandise to take a piece of Fergburger home with you. You can eat their burgers for breakfast, lunch, and dinner with the menu catering for the three main meals.

Finish off your burger experience with a sweet treat from Patagonia Chocolates or Cookie Time Cookie Bar.

For the fine dining experience there are many fine dining restaurants to tempt even the fussiest palate.

Accommodation in Queenstown can be among the most expensive in the country. There are at least 7 backpackers in town priced between $19-250.00 a night depending on your budget.

Juicy Snooze has a great deal from $43.00 a day. No sour faces at squeezing this price down because it's as low as it gets. Unless you prefer Huka Lodge at $25.00 a night.

A short stroll to shops and a 10-minute walk to some of Queenstown's popular attractions. Both these backpackers have Wi-Fi and free parking as well as the usual backpacker amenities.

If you want a deal with a hot tub, try Pinewood Lodge at $57.00 a night, this price won't dip into your budget too much. Stay at managed campgrounds where all the facilities you need are provided.

You are spoilt for choice with the nightlife in Queenstown. A unique bar experience is Minus 5 ICE BAR. Book your 30-minute slot in this Winter chiller and get 2 cocktails or 2 shots for $40.00. Entry is by booking a slot only at a further cost. Early bookings during the day are cheaper than after 10.00pm in the evening. A night spot with a chilled vibe.

Queenstown clubs and bars often have live music or D.J's for those wanting to pull an all-nighter. You can bar hop in central Queenstown to discover hidden laneways with the best and busiest clubs.

Queenstown restaurants offer a range of cuisine, from contemporary New Zealand fare using the fresher local produce, to delicious ethnic food or quick bites on the go. Explore your options.

Queenstown is the party hub of the country. 1876 is the go-to party place for locals and backpackers alike. The budget conscious will love the $4.00 happy hour menu and the $5 wine and beer deals too. This combination is enough to draw a crowd.

The London is party central if you enjoy pizza and dancing in an energetic atmosphere and the D.J's really get the party started after 10.00pm. The London is a large venue, perfect for special events.

Do you want to ride a huge mechanical bull or play pool or shuttle board, then head to Cowboys. It's a late-night place and busy after midnight.

For a good old fashioned pub crawl, Kiwi Crawl offer their standard 5 bar crawl every Tuesday through to Saturday. For $25 plus drinks, get home safety with their sober driver. For the Ice Bar crawls, $35.00 plus drinks is a great night out.

Price List for Accommodation & Main Activities

Bungy Jump $174.50 Adult

Arrowtown & Glenocy Free Spend

Hydro Attack $145.00 for 15 mins Adult

TSS Earnslaw $70.00 for 1.5 hours Adult

Luge From $64.00 - $72.00 Adult

Gondola From $46.00 - $160.00

Minus 5 ICE BAR $20.00 - $85.00 + Drinks Adult

Kiwi Crawl $25.00 - $35.00 + Drinks Adult

Juicy Snooze From $43.00 pn

Huka Lodge $25.00 pn

Pinewood Lodge $57.00 pn

Nomads $108.00

Day 25: Milford Sound & Te Anau

This is a flying visit to one of New Zealand's most breath-taking regions. Consider this a rest day if you need to. Milford Sound is a relaxing contrast to Queenstown. It takes a while to get there but it's totally worth the trip.

The Sounds are best experienced up close via a boat

cruise. Cruise up to the Bowen Falls, which are 160 metres high. Some boats have underwater viewing observatories. Look out for penguins, dolphins, and whales. Pack a lunch and drink to enjoy your day.

Spend the night in Te Anau and see the Glow worm Caves. Grab a quick bite to eat and turn in for an early start on the next leg of your trip.

Price List for Accommodation & Main Activities

Milford Sound Cruise & Underwater Observatory 3 hours From $119.00   Adult

Te Anau Glow-worm Caves $99.00 Adult

Tasman Holiday Park $44.00 - $166.00 pn

Day 26 – 27: Southland & Stewart Island

Arriving in Invercargill New Zealand's Southernmost city, enjoy the Tuatara House at the local museum or take a stroll around the gardens, aviary, or duck ponds of Queens Park. Stay overnight in Invercargill. At the Central City Camping park, you will find everything you need for a comfortable night. Sample some world-famous

Bluff oysters with chips and salad for dinner and wash it down with a beer or two.

Catch the ferry to Stewart Island from the Buff Visitor terminal. Open 7 days, ferries depart daily for Stewart Island. This trip can be done as a day trip or an overnighter. Time constraints may make a day trip a more practical option.

Stewart Island, is New Zealand's third largest island, located 30km south of the South Island, across the Foveaux Strait. Stewart Island can be reached by ferry which takes an hour.

Stewart Island is a bit colder year-round but not unpleasantly so in Summer. There is an abundance of things to do and see in Stewart Island. The permanent population today is around 480.

When Covid shut the world down to travellers, and lockdowns kept us all indoors, many people were disappointed to have holiday plans cancelled. In time the lockdowns lifted, and domestic flights picked up. New Zealander's were encouraged to explore their own back yard and go to places domestically that they had never been to before. Stewart Island came into view as a place to visit.

First time visitors couldn't get enough of the scenery and beauty this jewel destination had to offer. A main highlight of this trip is a 10-day sojourn of the Tin Range overlooking Port Pegasus for visitors with more time to explore the area.

If you are flying into the Island, a Cessna aircraft will deposit you on a short air strip of a low tide beach at remote Doughboy Bay on the western side of the island. A sheltered DOC hut is just a short stroll in from the beach. Later, in the evening you can catch a fabulous natural lightshow, the Aurora Australis, or Southern Lights.

Early Māori believed the light show was caused by the glowing campfires of their ancestors, trying to keep warm in the great land of snow and ice to which they departed after death.

Captain Eber Bunker of the Yankee sealing ship Pegasus anchored off this Bay, naming it Doughboy Bay after the dumpling-like rocks of the Bay's entrance.

Before the DOC hut was built here, a cave further along the beach served as shelter for many travellers.

History of the area informs, a Japanese 'cave woman' Keiko Agatsuma resided in the cave in the late 1970s before being deported as an overstayer in 1979.

All over the sand dunes creeping herbs like dense mats were dotted amongst the golden pingao. If tramping or hiking is your first love, there is an 8 hour walk over Adams Hill to Mason Bay.

Be aware the higher you go the muddier the track gets, to the point where muddy black ooze can reach thigh height. You are not going to come out of that walk clean by any standard.

You will be kept company on the track by flocks of kakariki chattering away in the overhead trees. If you keep quiet coming down to Mason Bay, you may spot one in the undergrowth. They scurry away at the first hint of noise. Whitetail deer is another future of the landscape that harbours Stewart Island's wildlife.

Coming down from this trail, you can catch a boat from Freshwater Landing out across Paterson Inlet to region civilization in Oban. There is a sprinkling of houses among the bush and the township in Oban, which is Gaelic for little Bay.

Many of the check-ins off the ferry land at the South Sea Hotel situated on the waterfront of Oban. The South Sea Hotel was originally built in 1926 to replace Oban House. This hotel is the hub of the settlement and is the main social centre of the Island.

This quaint cottage like hotel across the road from Halfmoon Bay, has an adjacent annex, and is a 4-minute walk from the ferry and 1km from Butterfield Beach. It boasts its own restaurant, free parking, free WIFI and beach access, Bar, and takeaways.

Southern Lights

Have a meal & a beer at the South Sea Hotel

Check out the beach

Hike the many trails on offer

Bird Watching

Stay in a DOC hut on an overnight hike

Take a scenic Stewart Island Road Tour + Wildlife Cruise

Arriving in Invercargill, bed down for the night at Central City Camping Park before catching the ferry the following morning. On Stewart Island, there is a backpackers with all the modern conveniences.

Price List for Accommodation & Main Activities

Central City Camping Park $26.00 - $110.00 pn

Stewart Island Ferry Services $85.00 one-way Adult

Stewart Island Backpackers $40.00 - $70.00 pn

Scenic Stewart Island Road Tour/Cruise $150.00 Adult

Day 28 – 29: The Catlins & Dunedin

Returning from Stewart Island, take the 3-hour bus trip, north to Dunedin. On the way you will pass through the rugged wilderness of the Catlins. Here you can visit a fossilized forest where the trees were alive around 180 million years ago. Watch the Hector Dolphins, seals, and penguins.

Dunedin has a quirky city vibe, lots of wildlife and a castle. Larnach Castle is well-worth a visit, especially the gardens with their seasonal floral displays amongst a collection of New Zealand plants.

Dunedin is home to rare wildlife, not found in the rest of the country. Albatross breed in thee world's only breeding colony of the Royal Northern Albatross. Dunedin is home to skinks, the tuatara lizard and 17 species of native birds.

Enjoy a locally brewed beer at the Emersons brewing Company, guided tour

Visit port Charmers for a mix of heritage, cafes, and galleries

Dunedin Street Art Walking Tour

Explore Dunedin's stunning beaches – St Clair is popular for surfing, Brighton Beach for swimming

Travel through time at Otago Museum or Toitu Otago Settlers museum

Guided Literacy Walking Tour

Olveston Historic Home

Botanic Gardens

Cycling

Mountain Biking trails – 1 Day up to 5 Day trips.

Surfing

There is lots of choice depending where you want to be situated. Near the beach, in the snow or right in the middle of the action. There is something to suit everyone. In the city is, On Top Backpackers. Don't break the law or you will find yourself at the Law Courts Backpackers. For a touch of heritage try the Manor House Backpackers.

Do you have a taste for the unusual the Chalet Backpackers may be your home away from home. Outside the CBD is Leith Valley Touring park or the Dunedin Holiday Park.

Megazone Entertainment Centre hits the top of the list with laser tag, mini golf 12 holes and jungle themed. Virtual Reality games, and the Game shop has board games. All this alongside a bar.

If it's naughty you are after, try Stilettos Revue Bar for

late night adult entertainment

Dinner, drinks, Dancing, Dunedin has it all. Pool Bars, Sports bars, and Night Clubs.

Are you feeling lucky? Try the Dunedin casino, featuring ornate gaming rooms, electronic machines and an upscale restaurant and live performances.

There is so much choice in Dunedin's nightlife, there is sure to be something to please all tastes and interests.

Price List for Accommodation & Main Activities

Larnach Castle $18.50 Adult

Emersons Brewing Company Tour $28.00 Adult

Dunedin Street Art Tour $30.00 Adult

Otago Museum Free

Toitu Otago Settlers Museum Free

Botanic Gardens Free

Olveston Historic Home $22.00 - $24.00 Adult

Guided Literacy Walking Tour $25.00 - $35.00 Adult

On Top Backpackers $29.00 - $79.00 pn

Chalet Backpackers $24.00 - $80.00 pn

Leith Valley Touring Park $70.00 pn

Dunedin Holiday Park $63.00 pn

The Law Courts Hotel $90.00 pn

Manor House Backpackers From $19.00 pn

Day 30 – 32: Lake Tekapo & Christchurch

Nearing the end of the month-long trip, Christchurch is the final destination on the itinerary.

Allow at least 3 days for this inspiring city to enjoy the wonders and the resilience of the people and the place. If you arrive in the Winter months of May to August, just remember warm clothing for this 'chilly bin' of New Zealand. Temperatures dip from 0 to 12 degrees.

The scars from the 2011 earthquake are evident

everywhere. This day is etched on the memories of Cantabrians indelibly. The loss for many was huge. 285 people perished on February 22nd at 12.51pm. The scars of the land and the people are still healing and there are many stories of heroism from that day.

The best place to learn about this sobering experience is Quake City, at the Canterbury museum. You will not come away from that exhibition the same as when you walked in. Quake City is an interactive experience to give viewers a real sense of what it was really like that day. It charts the events leading up to February 22nd

At 4.35am on September 4th, 2010, a magnitude 7.1 quake struck Christchurch damaging properties, land, and buildings. There was no loss of life as a direct result of the quake, but there was a massive clean-up job for property owners. Aftershocks of 5.6 were felt at 4.56am followed by more in the coming days.

Visit Quake City to learn about the affects to people, property, and livelihoods. Hear the stories and interact with the experience.

The International Antarctic Centre is a must-see experience. Situated 15 minutes from the city, using a local bus, this modern-day interactive Antarctic gives visitors a taste of life on this unique continent.

Experience an Antarctic storm, mix with the penguins and the huskies. Go off road in a Haglund. The impacts of humans on the wildlife on Antarctica damages the delicate ecosystems. Learn how you can help. An amazing day out for all ages.

Do you enjoy stargazing? Check out Lake Tekapo's Dark Sky Project for a chance to gaze at the stars and space through powerful telescopes. Free from light pollution this is the place to go to enjoy uninterrupted views of New Zealand night skies.

Another exciting day out is 'the most French village' in New Zealand. Akaroa is full of historic landmarks, cafes, keepsakes, and craft shops. Shopping, here, is fun and quirky. To enjoy Akaroa fully you may want to stay overnight. This is where the Top 10 Holiday Park comes in handy for that impromptu night away.

Akaroa is 1.5 hours from Christchurch. It has stunning harbour views from most points and majestic mountains. The best way to see Akaroa is on foot but if you must have wheels under you, consider hiring a bike for the day or a few hours. The information centre will provide you with brochures and maps so you can decide where to go first. Sample the amazing French food eateries and go along to Barry's Bay Cheese, where they have preserved the original ways of making cheese for centuries. Every second day you can watch through the gallery window as the cheese is being made.

Visit the Akaroa museum as it tells the story of Akaroa with displays and an audio-visual presentation. To round your trip off take a harbour cruise to see the dolphins and the seals, and the penguins.

The City centre is vibrant and colourful. Hop aboard the famous historic city tram, hop off to visit the Arts centre for exhibitions and live performances. The Canterbury Museum to explore New Zealand's rich cultural and natural heritage. Visit the Christchurch Botanic Gardens. These sights are all in the CBD.

Pack up and take a domestic flight back to Auckland so you can fly out from the international airport there or if you wish and your tickets allow you, fly out from the international airport in Christchurch.

Backpackers on offer in Christchurch include Jailhouse

accommodation. No, not the real jail, but a backpackers with an original difference. It's floors are shaped like Alcatraz. You can escape a high price. No need to tunnel out, doors are unlocked. In the centre of the city is Urbanz backpackers, situated for those who want to be close to the city. In this backpackers the city is on your doorstep. You can't get closer than that. Another great option is Juicy Snooze, close to the Airport if you are staying one night before flying out. At the low price per night, you won't be squeezed for a good sleep.

Christchurch is rocking at night, and no that's not another earthquake. Eclectic bars, Clubs, and the Christchurch Casino. Dining at the Terrace, dancing the night away right until the last minute of your vacation. Quick! Don't miss your flight!

Price List for Accommodation & Main Activities

Quake City $16.00 - $20.00

International Antarctic Centre $49.00 - $95.00

Bike Hire Akaroa From $15.00 - $60.00

Top 10 Holiday Park Akaroa From $32.00pn

Jail House Backpackers $54.00pn per cell

Urbanz Backpackers $56.00 pn

Juicy Snooze Airport $59.00 pn

Alternative Cost-Effective Ways to see New Zealand on a Budget

Airbnb

Homestays are profiled on many accommodation sites, or the Airbnb web site. The country is littered with them in every region. Some are Farm stays in the country or an entire apartment or house available for use by travellers. Prices start from $40.00 per night up to $250.00 a night for a whole house. If backpackers are full this could be your next best option.

Housesitting

For a small yearly fee, you can join house sitting web site, such as Trusted House sitters or Kiwi House sitters. You make a profile, telling all about yourself and your house-sitting preferences. Homeowners either contact you or you apply for the range of house sits available around the dates of your trip. The best part about looking after someone's property and pets is it is usually free to live except for food, travel, and activities. This is not a bad way to travel when you are on a budget but there is some responsibility for property and animals.

If you look after the pets and make sure they are fed and watered as per instructions, you will get an excellent reference from the homeowner that you can display on your profile. Other homeowners see the good recommendations and in come the offers of house sitting for the duration of your trip, and you can choose based on the dates of which region you will be based. Free accommodation means more money for fun and adventures.

Budget Motels

These are okay in a pinch, say if there was no vacancies in the backpackers for your specified dates. They are dearer than hostels and can dent the budget if you need to use them too often or they are priced out of reach of your wallet. Try not to get caught on the hop and make sure you have all accommodation requirements sorted before you come to New Zealand.

Work for Trade

Before you even think about this, you need to ensure you have working holiday visas and rights to work in New Zealand. If you don't have the correct visas when you land, this option is off the table. I cannot stress enough; it is your responsibility to have the correct visas.

However, a few hours work each day, may involve some farm work, or childcare, and hospitality. The usual agreement in these situation is 4 hours of work 5 days a week, traded for free accommodation and sometimes food. You could be gardening, fruit picking or cleaning.

Many travellers do this to keep their costs down and

save some money. In addition, you get valuable learning in the culture of New Zealand through first-hand experience. You stay with a host family from 2-6 weeks, they learn of your country and culture, and you learn of their experience and family culture.

You can even work at the hostel where you are staying on reception or housekeeping in return for a free bed. Plus, you get to find out what it is like to live long term in a hostel here. You will learn what we do as a country and as individuals to keep our country green and healthy for our visitors.

Sustainability & You (The Tourist)

The New Zealand government has enacted legislation such as the Resource Management Act 1991. It was a landmark piece of legislation , being the first to adopt the principle of sustainability. In January 2020, the New Zealand Upgrade Programme was announced with a focus on climate change. In 2019, the Zero Carbon Act was passed, with a goal of carbon neutrality by 2050.

The following is 13 amazing ways, you, the tourist can help promote sustainable travel. Therefore, you have a role as travellers:

• To come to New Zealand, take non-stop flights, where

possible. Take-offs and landings cause the most of a plane's carbon emissions, in addition to emitting a lot of heat.

• Go green, In your accommodation ask them not to change your sheets and towels every day. Turn off the air conditioning, heater, and electronic gadgets when you leave the room. Also stay in accommodation that have recycling programmes in place and abide by them.

• When traveling, travel with reusables like reusable water bottles, travel mugs, a cloth shopping bag for groceries, and containers for leftovers, avoid using single use disposables.

• Educate others by spreading awareness, leading by example. This helps drive long-term change on a systematic level.

• When traveling to a new place, support their local restaurants and cafes, as opposed to ordering from the fast-food giants. Supporting local means, you are sampling locally sourced ingredients and trying traditional food.

• Support legislation that promotes sustainable

tourism. It is up to us to ensure that more is done to protect this planet and its wildlife and humans.

• When you visit a new place, be sure to support their ventures by buying some of their souvenirs. By doing this you will be promoting the authentic artisans and their locally hand-crafted items. Check for local items that have some sort of value, such as ceramics, art, and textiles. You will be injecting money into the local economy, promoting peoples' work and creating more jobs for the locals.

• Walk wherever possible. Walking is the most basic and convenient way of exploring a new place. It reduces your carbon footprint.

• If you bring friends or family to New Zealand, ask them not to bring plastics, but to bring and use reusable items and reusable cloth shopping bags.

• Take care of heritage sites. Don't litter and take your rubbish with you to dispose of later. Don't graffiti or sit on the monuments. Look but do not touch. This way they will be there for others to view in the future.

• Respect the practices of the locals, when people are praying in churches, mosques or temples be discreet.

Wear decent clothing when visiting these places and abide by any established dress code.

• Don't use vulgar language when with the locals or doing anything that may cause offense. Always leave a place better than you found it.

• Make sustainable tourism the new normal, not just once but every time. Most importantly practice sustainability at home in your daily life. The planet will thank you for it.

Green Energy Accommodation

There are many ways to leave a tiny footprint in your travels, let's turn to sustainable accommodation. For the budget conscious there is a wide choice of eco-friendly backpackers' accommodation available.

• From $60.00 per night, come and stay at Egmont Eco Leisure Park in central New Plymouth. Tents and Campervans are welcome starting at $22.00 per night

• The Tree House set next to the peaceful Hokianga Harbour for the tourist touring the Far North. The small price is from $32.00 per person per night.

• In Auckland, The Attic, voted Auckland's Most Popular Hostel 4 Years in a row. From $56.00 per night for a clean, comfortable sleep in an eco-friendly environment.

This is just a small sample of eco-friendly accommodation on offer in New Zealand. You can go onto your favourite booking site to find Green Energy Accommodation anywhere in New Zealand.

Background of NZ's Sustainability

When thinking of New Zealand, images of clean, green, and pure come to mind for most people. Natural landscapes, sparkling rivers, vast and green land, unblemished beaches, an easy-going lifestyle, and fantastic living standards. A lack of pollution is a supporting factor in New Zealand's stunning reputation around the world.

However, New Zealand is not immune to threats of pollution and carries a huge ecological burden from negative effects of tourism and environmental issues. New Zealand is facing a huge clean-up bill today, after rioters' camped out on the Houses of Parliament frontage for 23 days. The last of the rioters were finally removed on Wednesday 02/03/2022.

Before they were removed, they had dug trenches into the lawns and gardens, pitched tents, bought in food trucks, and parked their vehicles illegally blocking surrounding streets. Parliamentary Services did provide them with Port-a-loos because they were pouring their bodily waste in our sewer systems.

You can imagine the smells after 23 days. During this time sickness, including Covid 19 raced through their camp like wildfire and the stench and violence of some of the riotous people, closed businesses, and schools in the area.

Having pitched tents and desecrated the grounds and monuments commemorating Anzac day Heroes and graffitiing others, a 500 strong Police team in riot gear pounced early one morning after giving every opportunity for rioters to leave peacefully and orderly.

The ensuing melee injured 5 Police officers as protesters set fire to trees, playgrounds and land and gardens and threw concrete paving stones at Police. In all Police arrested 100 people but managed to clear the area.

Left behind was a blacked, charred piece of land with remnants of clothing, tents and camping equipment with smoke curling out for 4 blocks. 50-100 cars were towed and confiscated.

The clean-up bill for this environmental disaster scene is picked to be at least 7 figures. The demands of the rioters were not met and were not even discussed between them and government officials while their illegal occupation was taking place. They were given the option to leave and then discuss their concerns but chose not to comply. So, a lot of environmental damage that did not need to happen, occurred for nothing.

Police continue to investigate to ensure that people who deliberately thumbed their noses at the law will be taken to account. Many of the rioters needed hospital treatment for illness gained from the 23 day stand in and Police say, the smell at the hospital followed the protesters there. I feel for the hospital cleaners.

Despite incidences like the one described above, New Zealand when compared with most other countries, still holds its own in cleanliness. Its location in the Pacific and stringent government policies and low population densities contribute to the countries preservation.

For years the onus has been on the people to preserve this functional paradise as a whole and they have been successful. With a population just shy of 5 million, New Zealand is in the top 20% of least densely populated countries. Overpopulation is detrimental to any environment.

New Zealand's history is built on a respect for the land and the environment. Māori believe that certain areas and objects are sacred. Māori places value on nature itself as they see gods in natural phenomena.

Kaitiakitanga is a word by Māori describing their obligation to take care of the land – obligation meaning a necessity. Māori traditions have their roots in taking care of the environment.

Māori are deeply involved in tourism with New Zealand Māori Tourism being a prime example. They offer their knowledge to those who care about their environment. They place importance on Rangatiratanga (leadership) and whanaungatanga (nurturing) relationships between Māori and visitors, showing visitors the importance of Māori traditions for the benefit of the land and the environment.

Tourists are found to respect the ethos of our country and are aware of the consequences of littering or leaving 'hazardous' waste. Before the advent of Covid tourist numbers to New Zealand were up to 4 million a year and was expected to rise.

Tiaki, a sustainability campaign aimed at youth, lays out the principles for locals and tourists to "Be Prepared, Show Respect, and Keep NZ clean." Tiaki aims to reduce its absolute greenhouse gas emissions by 25% by 2025.

Crime & Safety

Apart, from unruly protesters, New Zealand has a low crime rate, compared to other countries, but it is not entirely crime free. Listed below are ways you can keep yourself safe while travelling here. Firstly, the emergency number for fire, police or ambulance is 111 and is free.

• Make sure someone always knows where you are and when you will return.

• Don't walk alone at night and don't walk through

unlit areas.

- Don't carry lots of valuables on your person, only your phone, wristwatch, small amounts of cash. Leave everything else under lock and key at your accommodation.

- Be aware around other people, don't accept drinks from strangers or leave your drink unattended.

- Ensure you hide your PIN number when using ATM machines.

- Always lock your doors to accommodation and make sure windows are secure. Don't leave valuables, cameras, ATM cards, GSP devices visible in parked cars. Lock them in the boot.(trunk).

- Keep a record of the serial numbers of your cameras, laptops, and other valuables.

- Don't leave your belongings unattended in airports, train stations, bus or ferry terminals or other public spaces.

- Drive on the left-hand side of the road and give way

when you turn right.

- Do not use your mobile phone while driving, you will get a big fine for doing so.

- Never drive under the influence of alcohol or drugs and always wear your seatbelts.

- Report lost or stolen items or credit cards immediately.

These are just a few of the ways you can keep yourself and your valuables safe. If you have come on holiday with other people, travel together and try to go places together. Know where each other is and when, what time and where to meet up.

Crime rates in New Zealand are low to moderate, with petty theft and bag snatching, or vehicle break in being the biggest problem facing both locals and visitors. Keep your wits about you and take safety precautions and you should be fine.

Before you travel to New Zealand, learn what happens during a natural disaster. It's not that they happen every other week, but they do occasionally happen and you need to be prepared.

As travellers you need to know what hazards or natural disasters befall New Zealand. Earlier this guide touched on the Christchurch earthquake on February 22nd, 2011. In 2016 an earthquake rocked Kaikoura at a magnitude of 7.8. This occurred at 12.02am on 14th November 2016. Two people died in this event and 57 were treated for injuries.

New Zealand has a total land area of just 27,000 square kilometres, however, that land area coincides with the margin between the Pacific and Australian plates, which means New Zealand is very seismically active, many smaller earthquakes are unfelt.

Does this mean New Zealand will twist and turn during your visit? Possibly, however with seismic activity happening regularly, smaller earthquakes are hardly ever felt by people. If you find yourself caught up in a major event, follow all instructions from Civil Defence and Police.

In the case of volcanic eruptions, New Zealand has had one that killed and injured tourists and locals. Whakaari (White Island) had a volcanic eruption on 9th December

2019, killing 22 people and changing the lives of many others permanently.

Work Safe in New Zealand charged 13 parties, 10 organisations and three people for failing to follow health and safety rules. Survivors suffered serious burns to their skin and lungs and trauma. The island is closed to tourists.

While New Zealand has recorded some big storms, they are not frequent. The one I personally remember was Cyclone Bola in 1988, I was 25 and despite trees blown down and street signs. I walked to work. I worked in retail at the time, halfway there, I was picked up by one of our store reps, who saw me walking in the wind and rain. I was young but also stupid back then. The clean-up bill for that weather event was $111 million. There have been other major storms in New Zealand, this one sticks in my memory more than any others.

Floods are a common occurrence. On 5th February 2022 651 people were evacuated from their homes in Westport. Heavy rain over 48 hours coincided with a King tide. Flood waters from raised rivers closed state highways cutting Westport off by road and knocked out power and phones.

Pets were rescued and housed overnight at a temporary animal shelter with staff flying in from other areas to look after them. Pets and owners were reunited as residents were allowed back to their homes after 48 hours.

On average there is 3000-4000 wildfires in New Zealand each year. Up to 99% of wildfires are caused by humans with burn offs, rubbish fires, bonfires and fireworks and barbecues and equipment like electric fences.

Between heavy wet weather and earthquakes hill sides can crack and shear off burying properties and damaging roads, railway lines and farms. Landslides are more common in New Zealand than other countries because of the steep land, weak layers, and high rainfall.

Civil Defence is a volunteer-based emergency response organisation. Civil Defence supports the frontline emergency services. They also carry out community support activities at most disaster events, both locally and nationally.

Don't live or travel in fear that an emergency situation

may occur, just be aware and be prepared in the unlikely event. Enjoy your travels and sights off the main travel drags and you can discover some real gems.

Undiscovered Gems & Off the Beaten Track

In keeping with the sustainability message, visiting places that have not been inundated with travellers to much is a great way to see more of the country and places not visited as often as the main attractions that bring visitors in.

Taranaki (New Plymouth)

New Plymouth, on the West Coast of the North Island is in the province of Taranaki, like no other, as the slogan goes.

Taranaki (New Plymouth) is rich farming country, with Mountains on one side and the Tasman sea on the other. New Plymouth has a beautiful man-made park right in the centre of the city. Pukekura Park covers 52 ha and is one of New Zealand's prime botanical gardens. The park has a fernery and display houses as well as being home to the TSB Bowl of Brooklands and Brooklands Zoo. There are tearooms and Kiosk, row boats on the lake, guided or self-guided walks. The park also features a waterwheel and a children's playground among plenty of other sights and the best part is it is all free.

During the Christmas and New Year period the park is arrayed with colourful lights. There is also a nightly programme of performance and dance. The Festival of lights as it is known attracts visitors from all over the world and is free to everyone.

If you are looking for more active attractions, explore the beaches around the city, from Fitzroy beach where you can surf the hollow waves to the southern edge of New Plymouth at Back beach where you can catch great swells. Back beach hosts a New Year Summer Carnival every year. Try the local food, fun and markets.

If hiking is more your thing Mt Taranaki in the middle of Egmont National Park offers walks and hikes for all levels of abilities. The Coastal walkway in the centre of the city spans from the Port to Bell block, 20 minutes by car north of New Plymouth. Walkers can get on and off at various places along the walkway.

Summer is hot with temperatures from 25-28 degrees. Winter, on the other hand, is wet, windy, and wild, with frosts and wind from the mountain and off the sea so it gets very chilly here in the Winter, from 12-15 degrees.

Travel further around the coast to Opunake. Stop on the way at the historic site of Parihaka. In the 1800s Parihaka Māori staged a peaceful protest over the Crown's confiscation of their lands. In Opunake visit the local craft stores and the Cape Egmont Replica Lighthouse. A five-day stay would allow you to engage with any road trips round the coast and take in inner city New Plymouth and it is super easy to pick up keepsakes of your time in Taranaki.

For all your sightseeing accommodation needs, New Plymouth offers some great bargains. Starting with Ariki Backpackers right in the centre of town with views of the waterfront and the wind wand. Braemar Motor Inn, 1.2km from the city. With views of Mt Taranaki, Egmont Eco Leisure Park & Backpackers is a fabulous place to stay if you want uninterrupted views of the mountain.

Price List for Accommodation

Ariki Backpackers From $71.00pn Adult

Braemar Motor Inn From $99.00 pn Adult

Mt Taranaki Egmont Eco Leisure Park From $75.00 Adult

Waitomo Caves

Between Hamilton in the Waikato and Te kuiti in the King Country is an attraction called Waitomo Caves. Waitomo village as it is known, has an extensive underground cave system. Thousands of glow worms light up the caves. The Ruakari Cave, which is the largest, features waterfalls and limestone formations.

The most popular cave combo, Glow worm cave and Ruakauri cave, pay just $100.00 per adult or for $40.00 more enjoy the triple cave combo with the addition

Aranui Caves.

Glide under thousands of magical glow worms on the world-famous boat ride. In these caves there is over 125 years of cultural and natural history. Where better to get a natural glowing history lesson in real time. The boat guides will share their knowledge of this awesome environment, sharing the caves' historical and geographical significance.

World renowned and drawing thousands of visitors, both local and international, the glow worm caves are high up on traveller's bucket list. The legend of Waitomo began 30 million years ago with the creation of limestone at the bottom of the ocean. Now these limestone formations are at the top of New Zealand's natural wonders and treasures.

The name Waitomo comes from Māori words wai (water) and tomo (hole). If you are into adventure and adrenaline rush, try black water rafting, you will crawl, swim and float through the caves on a rubber tube. Or you could abseil or Zip-line through the darkness.

There are a myriad of free walks and sights around Waitomo, Managapohue Natural Bridge, Ruakauri Bush walk, Marokopu falls or Ed Hillary Walkway to name some of the many highlights of the area. Don't leave without having a good look around and enjoy the hospitality on offer here.

Otorohanga Kiwi House

Twenty minutes south of Waitomo is Otorohanga, where you can visit our national icon, the Kiwi, head to Otorohanga Kiwi House. This is home to some species of our native bird, the Kiwi and to many of New Zealand's native birds.

One species of Kiwi, the Brown Kiwi weighs between 1.5-3kgs. Kiwi's come out to feed at night and sleep during the day. They like dark, moist habitats. They can be found in forested areas of the North Island, Little Barrier Island, Kapiti Island, and forest areas south of Palmerston North.

South Island Gem

Do you want to know a secret? Tucked away at Whekenui Bay near the entrance of Tory Channel, lies the most exquisite jewel. New Zealand's only Paua Pearl

Farm. Pearls native, only to New Zealand.

Would you like to know more? Arapawa Blue Pearls Farm is a beauty with more than meets the eye.

How? Situated on the sparkling shores of the Marlborough Sounds this little gem crafts gemstones of the highest quality.

Arapawa Blue Pearls Farm is a picturesque Island, in the Marlborough Sounds at the top of the South Island. Imagine staying on an Island a world away from the hustle and bustle of daily life. The only access across to the Island is by boat or water Taxi for the 1.5-hour trip. You can also book the mail boat cruise from Picton, twice a week on Tuesday and Friday. For a quick trip from Wellington, indulge in a helicopter ride.

The owners offer a unique trio of experiences, legendary eco-friendly hospitality, and accommodation. 360 hectares of panoramic views, outdoor recreation, and a learning experience like no other, how the pearl gets from Paua seed to breathtaking jewelry.

Sustainably is the backbone of the business. Paua is sourced locally from the waters surrounding the farm.

The recent earthquakes have interrupted the reseeding Project by causing a huge rise along the coast and most of the juvenile habitat of Paua was wiped out. Partnerships were formed with another group, on reseeding the area.

While the outcomes of the work are passionate and indulgent, simple methods are used to create a haven for the Abalone Paua. This little piece of paradise has been teamed with a vibe of celebration and a sharing of enjoyment and passion, with you, the visitors, who want to learn the magnificent story of resilience, beauty, and symbolism behind the Abalone Paua.

There is a rich layer of history, at Whekenui Bay, of Māori settlement, World War II battles, evidenced by the gun emplacements. Whekenui Bay was the Centre of the whaling industry in Marlborough Sounds from the 1820's to the mid 1960's. On the trip from Picton to the bay you will see mussel, salmon and oyster farms that took over after the last of the whaling stations closed.

For two decades the whaling station went from a shack to a large factory that processed tons of whale carcasses. The factory ran off a huge generator that used more power than the whole of the Marlborough region combined and employed 45 workers. It all came to an end in 1964 and today the Perano whaling station stands as a monument to the hard-working men who built a business from scratch and made it into a lifestyle that sustained them for years.

In 2001 the first real venture into Paua Farming, started with just 4 tanks. After the earthquakes there were 20 large tanks from which to begin the reseeding process again. This began the resettlement of 4,000,000 swimming larvae for the area, to be released at 8 months old, a project another group had been trying to get up and running for many years.

Today there are 250 Paua Farm tanks with Paua with pearls growing in them. Pearls are grown from wild Paua harvested from the rocky shores of the Cook Strait. They are now producing the highest quality Abalone (Paua) Pearls in the world.

Each pearl is like a snow flake, in that each one is different and naturally grown so colour may vary from one to the other.

Holiday Accommodation

On offer is four distinctive 'kiwi bach' style accommodation options. Choose the one right for you, for a family holiday, a romantic getaway, or a group adventure.

School Cottage

Starting with the School Cottage, which is the remodeled school where the whaler's children were educated. Today the School Cottage is still the same purposed built building, altered into living accommodation for guests It is a landmark of the rich history of this area.

This cozy self-contained little nook sleeps six. There is one set of double bunks and one set of single bunks. There is a fold down bed for an extra person.

School Cottage features, open plan living, fully equipped kitchen and a Webber BBQ. Freezer space is available. Separate shower and toilet facilities. Separate laundry with washing machine and clothes dryer. A heat pump for heating/air conditioning. A private deck with surround panoramic views.

School Cottage is pet friendly subject to approval before arriving.

The pricing structure is as follows:

Summer (October to May inclusive)

$210.00 up to six people per night.

$22.00 per night for each additional person if extra camping is required.

$50.00 per night for each pet (pets subject to prior approval).

Off Season (June to September inclusive)

$190.00 up to six people per night

$22.00 per night for each additional person if extra camping is required.

$50.00 per night for each pet (pets subject to approval prior to arrival).

Minimum stay is two nights. Dingy and mooring is included in the Tariff. One night's payment confirms your booking. All linen is supplied. All Price include GST. Enjoy the sun, the beach, and the views of this well-appointed Cottage.

Little Colonsay Beach House

How about your own private beach? The latest addition to our accommodation fleet, is a beach house perched right near the beach, so close you can hear the waves and smell the salt air. This is what a true kiwi bach experience is all about. A short stroll and you can dip your toes in the water.

Little Colonsay Beach House was built in 1952 for the engineer at Perano whaling Station, David Cormick, who helped to design and build the large, metal, cylinder shaped tanks used for delivering the whale oil to Picton. These tanks remain at the Whaling station site today.

This sunny abode gets day round, year-round sun, even in the Winter. A self-contained beach house which sleeps 12 people, has two Queen size beds, One double bed and six single beds, along with a separate sleepout.

The kitchen has an electric oven with a gas stove top, a microwave and a dishwasher and a Webber BBQ. Separate laundry with washing machine and dryer. There is the addition of a new billfold door and sliding door, opening from the lounge onto the deck.

The sleepout located behind the house includes an extra-large shower, designed for divers to put on their wetsuits, and to new toilets with a double hand basin.

Little Colonsay Beach House is Pet friendly subject to approval prior to arrival.

The pricing structure is as follows:

Summer (October- May inclusive)

$420.00 per night up to five people.

$22.00 per night for each for each additional person.

$50.00 for each pet (pets subject to prior approval).

Indulge in a couple's summer season: $200.00 per night, up to two people.

Off Season (June – September inclusive)

$380.00 up to 5 people

$22.00 per night for each additional person

$50.00 per night for each pet. (Pets subject to prior approval).

Minimum stay of 2 nights. Dinghy and mooring are included in the Tariff. One night's payment confirms your booking. All linen supplied. All prices include GST.

Gunyah

The Arapawa Homestead, or Gunyah as it is known, is the original house built in 1945 by Joe and Patty Perano as their retirement home. Refurbished to retain its 1940's character, the Homestead is fully equipped. It is private and cozy.

Gunyah sleeps up to 13 people and includes a fold-out bed and a cot for younger children.

Gunyah is an Aboriginal name and means, sheltered spot or sacred spot. The Homestead is sheltered from the wind which goes up and over the bluff.

The main bedroom is furnished with an antique walnut bedroom suite that includes a double bed with a feather duvet and a single bed for an extra guest. This room offers wide, sweeping views of Tory Channel and the West Head.

The Homestead is suitable for children, the second bedroom contains two sets of single bunks with duvets. This room has stunning ocean views.

Gunyah has a sleepout containing a queen size bed, two sets of single bunks, plus a shower and a toilet. The sleepout doubles as the laundry, with sinks, washing machine and dryer. The sleepout has a spacious wooden deck which catches the afternoon sun. There is also a small fridge.

The inside bathroom has a deep comfortable bath, with a separate toilet. The Homestead has full amenities with everything you need for a comfortable stay. In the kitchen there is modern appliances, including a microwave oven, fridge/freezer, and a bread maker and a Webber BBQ. The living area has a wood burner, ideal for those cold Winter nights and a sound system to play your mobile devices.

The views feature a never-ending stream of ferries that travel past, on their route from Picton to Wellington and return. The ferries travel so close to wave out to the people on deck.

Gunyah is pet friendly subject to prior approval before arriving.

The pricing structure is as follows:

Summer (October – May inclusive)

$330.00 per night up to five people.

$22.00 per night for each additional person

$50.00 per night for each pet (Pets subject to prior approval).

Off Season (June-September inclusive)

$270.00 per night up to five people.

$22.00 per night for each additional person.

$50.00 per night for each pet (Pets subject to prior approval).

We are offering a Couple's Discount Special this Summer season: $200.00 per night for up to two people.

Minimum stay of two nights. Dinghy and mooring are included in the Tariff. One night's payment confirms your booking. All Linen is supplied. All prices include GST.

Do you want to bring a group to Arapawa Blue Pearl Island? Would you like to hold an event or a Wedding?

Now you can. We are offering the full and exclusive use of the Arapawa Homestead accommodation. You can sleep 31 people across our range of accommodation. The Arapawa Homestead, Little Colonsay House, Gunyah and the School Cottage are available for group functions.

The pricing structure is as follows:

Summer (October-May inclusive)

$850.00 up to 31 people.

Off-Season (June-September inclusive)

$850.00 up to 31 people.

Minimum stay 2 nights. Dinghy and mooring are included in the Tariff. One night's payment confirms your booking. All Linen supplied. All prices include GST.

For all accommodations you will need to bring your own supplies and clothing to the Island. There are no roads in or out or shops at hand. You can order your groceries from the mainland. The two supermarkets we order through:

Blenheim New World

New World uses Mark Jackson to courier the groceries to the Island.

Ph: 03 5209030

Jenny.woolley@newworld-si.co.nz

Picton Fresh Choice

Your supplies come in on the mail boat, with a charge of 5% of the total order to your grocery invoice. Add a $5.00 charge if it is a public holiday.

Order by 12.00 noon the day before the mail boat

delivery day

soundsorders@pictonfreshchoice.co.nz

There is something on offer for everyone. From a gentle walk to the whaling station (10 mins), or to the Loop track. This takes you around the farm to the top of the Island and take in the spectacular views of the outer sounds. If you are fortunate, you will catch a glimpse of Mt Taranaki. (5 km).

Back in the Bay, you can take a tour where you can see all the procedures that come into play when presenting Paua Pearl Farm. You can see what has been done in the past., what is being done now and where this might take Atapawa in the future. The tour takes 90 minutes.

There are Paua Pearls to show to you of all colors and grades. You can view jewelry that can be purchased here both in Gold and Sterling Silver, made by local jewelers in Marlborough. You can choose a pearl and have your own piece of jewelry designed to your tastes. No job to big or too small.

Atapawa is the only hatchery in New Zealand where they can plant baby Paua, During the tour watch how

Paua is spawned and the work that goes into this huge operation.

If you enjoy fishing, you can fish off our wharf in the early morning or later in the day as these are the best times.

There is a 4-wheeler side by side for hire ($80) subject to availability. A big attraction for the kids are our eels who live in our creek by the main house. They love to be fed fish or anything disposable. The eels are not for catching and eating, they are pets.

Weather permitting helicopters can arrive on our beach to collect or drop off guests to stay.

Turn your special occasion or event into an unforgettable experience. Hurry so you can tick this trip off your bucket list.

Hunting & Fishing Seasons

For all you hunters and gatherers out there who want to bag a duck or fish some trout. New Zealand has rules, laws, and regulations, governing what can be caught and when and size of catch both in number and individual size of each duck or trout.

These things matter for sustainability and to ensure the continues to be enough for everyone. Some forms of hunting need individual licenses as well as season periods.

So, for all you guys who dream of catching and cooking your own wild food, this section will be pertinent to you and your plans. Depending on which type of species of duck you want, local regions have their own rules.

For example, for a mallard or a grey duck, the main season is between 1 May to the 27th June. This is the same for all regions when there are mallard or grey duck. In Northland the daily bag limit is 12, Auckland/Waikato the daily bag limit is 10. Eastern areas are 6, Hawkes Bay is 8, Taranaki is 10 and Wellington is 10 daily bag limit.

This is one example for two species of duck here, for all others, for times, limits and regions. Fish and game regulates, game bird hunting throughout New Zealand. The regulations are amended each years to suit the changing sporting and environment conditions.

For most hunting and fishing activities you will need purchase a licence. For the example above, you can get a duck hunting licence for a day trip from $19.00 a day or a whole of season licence from $94.00.

Let's look at the process and logistics of coming from the US to New Zealand for Hunting. The devil is in the details and if you plan well the hunting experience will go well.

Planning starts with purchasing flights, don't forget to make it non-stop if possible. Next you need to apply for a NZ visitor's firearm licence by going to NZPO website and applying online. Check the varying airline regulations both in US and here, for carrying a firearm and notify the airline of intention to bring a firearm. Fill in the US Customs form 4457 for firearm.

Most important for Bio security checks at Customs in New Zealand clean all your back country gear. New Zealand has a unique set of native eco-systems and an economy based on agriculture and tourism. Our Island nation is concerned about making sure invasive species don't enter our borders.

On arrival in New Zealand, decide on a place to hunt, after clearing customs, head over to the NZPO kiosk and speak to the officer for confirmation of your visitor's firearm licence. You pay a fee in cash for your licence after proving you are permitted to have a firearm in the US.

Rent a car. This the easiest way to travel around New Zealand on a hunting expedition. The car rental can be done online before you leave the US. Getting your meat back to the US requires a butchers' receipt, obtain a certificate to export trophies and meat from DOC central office.

Have all the meat and trophies prepared and packaged professionally. Online fill out US fish and wildlife Service Form 13-77, importing fish and wildlife. Thoroughly clear all your hunting gear. There are fees to pay for the paperwork.

Fishing Regulations

You do not need a licence to Fish in the sea around New Zealand. However, you do need a licence for freshwater fishing in lakes or rivers. Visitors' to New Zealand can purchase a day non-resident licence for $34.00 for an adult. If you are fishing in Lake Taupo a day non-resident licence will set, you back $129.00.

In New Zealand you will need a licence to fish trout and salmon. There is a limit on size to keep the fish stock healthy. Size limits are there to protect the fish of spawning size before they are caught. Fishing seasons protect fish during spawning and limit the catch on heavily fished waters.

The main trout fly fishing season opens on the 1st of October and runs through until the end of April. There are some exceptions to these date so check out each region for local differences.

Under the Treaty Of Waitangi, Māori were given sovereignty over the waters and fish that live there. What this means is they have set fishing quotas on shellfish to maintain the sustainably of the fish stocks.

Crayfish, which most tourists would just love to try have to be no less than 216mm in size and 6 is the daily bag limit. Trout must be 35cm in length and the daily bag limit is 6. For Salmon, that is a rich and creamy fish must be 45cm long and 2 is the daily bag limit.

Shellfish is a delicacy in New Zealand and as such is very popular. Strict limits are imposed on gathering shellfish and boats and vehicles can be confiscated and big fines imposed for non-compliance.

- Kina 50 catch limit

- Muscles 50 catch limit

- Oysters must be 85mm to 125mm from the widest part with 50-250 catch limit.

- Paua must be 100mm and 10 is the daily catch limit

- Scallops have a daily bag limit of 20.

Preparing & Cooking Fish & Shellfish

Many people love oysters al natural' (raw) with a squeeze of lemon. If this makes you shudder, you can make a batter with 1 cup flour, ¾ cup milk, an egg, 2 teaspoons of baking powder and half a can of beer. Dredge them in this and deep fry and enjoy with a squeeze of lemon and a side of hot chips and salad.

Crayfish is better eaten at a fine dining restaurant where a good chef can do it justice. Be aware that it is expensive dining out. Well worth the price, however.

Trout is delicious baked and very simple. Salt and freshly ground pepper, A whole trout, 1 cup of sundried tomatoes, soft white breadcrumbs, Garlic, and mixed herbs, all easily bought from the local supermarket.

Fillet but don't skin the trout, lay the fillets out on a

baking tray, skin side down. Put sundried tomatoes, soft breadcrumbs, garlic, and mixed herbs into a kitchen whizz. Add oil from the sundried tomatoes and blend to a firm moist consistency. Add salt and pepper to taste.

Completely cover both fillets with the mixture and firmly mould to the fillet by hand. Bake for 15 minutes at 180 degrees C, then serve with lemon juice and a freshly tossed salad.

Salmon has a range of recipes to tempt. One of my favourites is Baked Salmon. Two salmon fillets covered in a garlic, lemon, parsley, and butter mix. Place salmon skin side down on a baking tray and cover both fillets. Bake for 15 minutes at 180 degrees C, then serve with baby potatoes and a tossed salad.

Kina is shellfish with a prickly outside shell. The idea is to get the fish meat from inside the shell. Insert a sharp pair of scissors into the centre of the kina shell. Wear a thick pair of gloves to avoid getting poked by the spines on the outside shell. Cut a hole in the kina big enough to fit a spoon inside the hole to scoop out the flesh.

Once you have the Kina tongues out, rinse thoroughly in salted water to clean. Traditionally Kinas are eaten raw, deep fried or baked in a pie.

Muscles are traditionally made into fritters and served with hot chips and salad. Make the same batter as for oysters without the beer and shallow fry. Paua is made into fritters also, with a cup of minced Paua, a small, chopped onion, parsley and mint, some lemon zest, ½ cup of self-rising flour and an egg. Mix all the ingredients together and season with salt and pepper. Heat a BBQ plate and add oil.

Drop large spoonful's on and cook until golden brown on both sides. Make sure they are cooked right through, as there is nothing worse than gooey batter. Serve with wedges of lemon and a tossed salad.

Scallops are best dredged in a beaten egg and rolled in breadcrumbs and deep fried. Serve with hot chips and a side salad.

Enjoy the treasure of New Zealand waters and beautiful landscapes, especially in the many National Parks.

New Zealand's National Parks

New Zealand has 13 National Parks. This include Tongariro National Park, Whanganui National Park, Egmont National Park, Kahurangi National Park, Nelson Lakes National Park, Able Tasman National Park, Arthur's Pass National Park, Paparoa National Park, Aoraki Mt Cook National Park, Mt Aspiring National Park, Westland Tai Poutini National Park, Fiordland National Park, & Rakiura National Park.

All 13 of them showcase more than 30,000 square kilometres of diverse, natural scenery ready to explore by foot, by car, by boat or by air. The hardest choice to make is which ones to explore while you are here. Here are 3 popular choices.

Tongariro National Park

Is the oldest National Park in New Zealand, located in the central North Island. It has been acknowledged by UNESCO as a World Heritage Site of mixed cultural and natural values. Tongariro National Park was the sixth National Park established in the World in 1887.

There are sights and activities to suit every age, interest, and ability.

Tongariro Alpine Crossing

If you are as fit as a buck rat and want a challenge, then this is for you. This hike is an 8-hour walk, climb, run down scree slopes and hike all rolled into one. The Grade is advanced. For a small fee transport will pick you up and drop you at the beginning of the Crossing and meet you at the other end at the DOC Hut when you emerge.

In the Summer remember to take at least 2 litres of

water, sunscreen, sunglasses, and a hat and your lunch. Take warm clothing too, because the weather can quickly change, thermals, warm hiking pants, socks, and proper hiking boots and a rain jacket In a small backpack carry your water, lunch and sunscreen, band aids for any blisters and any other items you may be advised to take for the day.

It is strongly recommended not to attempt the Crossing in the Winter. However, if you are crazy enough to do it at that time of the year, use the services of a qualified guide due to the extra dangers of the Crossing with deep snow and ice walls and fog and wind. Take everything you would take in the Summer, plus extra woolly socks, and woolen hats, along with eco plastic bags to carry any wet clothing.

Tongariro Northern Circuit 4 Days 41 km

This is an intermediate grade 4-day walk. The best time to go is late October to late April. This amazing walk encircles Mount Ngauruhoe, an active volcano in Tongariro National Park. You will see craters, explosion pits, lava flows, the emerald lakes, and wildflowers and waterfalls during the 4-day walk.

You will need to book and pay for your accommodation in the DOC Huts along the route in advance before you go. You can do this at the Whakapapa Village or any Hunting & Fishing or Outdoor recreation store in New Zealand. Check out the weather reports for the 4 days and any volcanic activity in the area.

Day 1, Whakapapa Village to Mangatepopo Hut 8.5 km

Beginning 100 m below the Whakapapa Village information centre, on today's hike you will see stream beds, volcanic views, and ancient lava flows. The final hour of this hike skirts around an old steam vent before reaching the Mangatepopo Valley track and the hut a while later.

Day 2, Mangatepopo Hut to Emerald Lakes to Oturere Hut 12.8 km

Today's steep climb rewards you with spectacular views of the Central Plateau in addition to the Blue and Emerald Lakes, which fill explosion pits. The brilliant colour is caused by volcanic minerals washing down from the thermal areas. From here the track descends down into the Oturere Valley where tonight's Hut will be waiting for you.

Day 3, Oturere Hut to Waihohonu Hut 7.5 km

The track, today, runs through a number of stream valleys and open fields. You will move around the foothills of Mount Ngauruhoe before walking through a Beech Tree valley and arriving at the Waihohonu Hut.

Day 4, Waihohonu Hut to Whakapapa Village, 14.3 km

Today's track steadily climbs to Tama Saddle, where there is a beautiful side trip to the Tama Lakes and two old explosion craters. Whakapapa village is two hours walk from here. After the first hour the track intersects with Taranaki Falls Loop walk – follow the track to the bottom to see the waterfall before following the stream to reach the village.

Round the Mountain Track 6 Days, 66.2 km

This hike is 6 days of tussock country and alpine herb fields, volcanic landscapes, and mountain peaks. It is an advanced grade track leading right around Mount

Ruapehu, one of the towering volcanic cones in Tongariro National Park.

Day 1, Whakapapa Village to Waihohonu Hut, 5 hours 30 minutes

Follow the track as it leads through tussock and shrubland to the Wairere stream. Pass through the mountain beech forest the base of the Taranaki Falls. Wind your way upwards to the Tama Saddle, before descending down to the Waihohonu Hut for the night.

Day 2, Waihohonu Hut to Rangipo Hut, 5 Hours

Today's track leads through the North Island only true desert and the most unique landscape in the Park. Explore wind sculptured sands, stark volcanic and amazing mountain views. Climb the Eastern side of Ruapehu on the way to Rangipo Hut.

Day 3, Rangipo Hut to Mangaehuehu Hut, 5 Hours 30 minutes

The track returns to the mountain beech forest. The trail crosses the magnificent Waihianoa Gorge, a giant fissure through the volcanic landscape. Climb uphill to

Mangaehuehu Hut, accommodation for the night.

Day 4, Mangaehuehu Hut to Mangaturuturu Hut, 4 Hours 30 minutes

Move through the alpine tussock and beech forest as you make your way downhill from the Hut. The track passes Rotokawa, alpine tarn featuring several species of wetland plants and a lava ridge covered in alpine herbs,

Day 5, Mangaturuturu Hut to Whakapapaiti Hut, 5 Hours 30 minutes

Today's track takes you across the Mangaturuturu River, past lakes and through river valleys. See the waterfalls that tumble down lava bluffs in the Whakapapaiti Valley.

Day 6, Whakapapaiti Hut to Whakapapa Village, 2 Hours 30 minutes

Continue down the Whakapapaiti River valley and move through groves of native kaikawaka and cabbage trees in the beech forests on your way back to Whakapapa village and the end of your 6-day hike.

The Round the Mountain track can be walked any time of the year, but the safest and most popular time is from November to May. This is a mountain wilderness area where the weather can change quickly, so come well prepared.

Nature Trails

A series of short nature trails around the lower slopes of the Park show the various habitats that are home to a diverse native flora and fauna and are a great way to get to know the Parks special places and stories. The National Park visitors centre is a good place to start exploring.

Waterfalls

Dramatic waterfalls are a specialty in the Park. See them on a number of amazing short walks including Taranaki Falls, Waitonga Falls, Silica Rapids and Tawhai Falls.

Skiing

Enjoy excellent skiing and snowboarding on Mount Ruapehu's ski fields. Whakapapa, Turoa and Tukino. For non-skiers, there is tobogganing and tubing or just drive up to take in the views.

New Zealand's Highest Café (Highly Recommended by a Local)

A scenic ride on a gondola at Whakapapa reaches New Zealand's highest café, Knoll Ridge, where you can enjoy scenic dinning in the Summer and the Winter. I have, personally, done this and can attest to both the gondola ride and the food at the top as epic. Don't take my word for it, try it for yourself.

Lord of the Rings Film Sites

Tongariro National Park's scenery had a starring role in Peter Jackson's Lord of the Rings Trilogy. Mount Ngauruhoe took centre stage and is now famous all over the world.

Price List for DOC Hut Accommodation

Hut Fees $15.00 per person per night Adult

Able Tasman National Park

This National Park perches on the coast near the top of the South Island. Forty minutes from Nelson, Able Tasman is New Zealand's smallest National Park. It is the perfect place to be for relaxation and adventure. Sandy beaches and granite and marble formations blend with regenerating native forests.

You can choose to explore the park from land, on the water, or in the air with tours operators offering cruises, shuttles, water taxi services, kayaking, Heli-tours and sailing catamarans.

Native wildlife is an essential part of the scenery Tui and Bellbirds sing the day away, shags and gannets dive for their dinner, fur seal line the rocks soaking up the sun on the edge of Tonga Island.

Classed as one of New Zealand's Great Walks, the Able Tasman Coastal Walk track has easy accessibility by boat. This means you can choose to walk some of the track and paddle the rest of leave the track after a day or two via water taxi.

Before you embark on this walk, remember to book your hut accommodation and transportation to and from the track in advance. This applies all year round. The track is easy to intermediate grade so walker of varying fitness can enjoy the track.

Using the services of a guide will bring the track and its scenery alive and add colour to the experience. The track is not a circuit track so transport will need to be booked and organised before you start.

Day 1, Marahau to Anchorage, 12.4km

Starting at the Marahau information kiosk, follow the causeway that crosses the estuary. From here, you'll pass through open country to Tinline Bay. The track rounds Guibert Point to Apple Tree Bay before crossing through beech forest with large kanuka trees. After Yellow Point the track heads inland, through small gullies before emerging into Torrent Bay, overlooking the coast and islands to the North. Go down into the bay where a hut and campsite awaits.

Day 2, Anchorage to Bark Bay, 12.1km

Cross the low ridge to Torrent Bay Estuary, this can be

crossed two hours either side of the high tide or a longer all tide track leads up and around the headland. At the Northern end the track climbs steadily before reaching a 47m-long suspension bridge strung above an inlet. The track takes you through coastal forest before dropping back down to the sea. Here, in Bark Bay is the Hut beside the Estuary.

Day 3, Bark Bay to Awaroa, 11.4km

Cross the Estuary or follow the all-tide track around the edge where you will climb steeply to a saddle. Walk through a Manuka forest coming out at the shore at Tonga Quarry. On Tonga island is a Marine reserve with fascinating underwater life. Stop to go snorkelling is highly recommended. Resuming the trial, you will come to Onetahuti Bay, cross the all-tide bridge and boardwalk. The track climbs up and over Tonga Saddle before winding down to Awaroa inlet and Awaroa Hut.

Day 4, Awaroa to Whariwharangi, 13km

Awaroa Estuary can be crossed a few hours either side of the low tide. The track drops into Waiharakeke Bay where an old timber mill used to be located. Going through more forest and beaches, you will eventually came to a look-out with fantastic views. The song of bellbirds, fantails, kereru, and tui will serenade you along the track. After crossing forests and beaches the track drops down into Whariwharangi Bay and accommodation in the hut, for the night on an old, restored homestead.

Day 5, Whariwharangi to Wainui, 5.5km

A much shorter hike takes you the end of the track and the car park. Here you meet your transport back to Marahau. For water taxi pick-ups hikers need to return to Totaranui via Gibbs Hill , a 3-hour walk.

There is so much to do in Able Tasman National Park, it pays to stay an extra couple of days to relax. Take in the buzzing city of Nelson with its arty vibe and café culture.

Price List for DOC Hut Accommodation

Hut Fees (NZ CIT & RES) $42.00 Adult

Hut Fees (INTNAT VISIT) $56.00 Adult

These fees are for the height of the Summer season, they get lower in the Winter months.

Aoraki Mount Cook National Park

Mt Cook is the highest mountain in New Zealand. Mt Cook helped Sir Edmond Hillary train and prepared for his conquest of Mt Everest. The Māori name for the Mountain, Aoraki, means 'cloud piercer'.

The national park is very accessible, State Highway 80 leads to Mt Cook village beside Lake Pukaki and provides a comfortable base for those undertaking alpine activities. Don't forget to join in with the amazing stargazing here. Mt Cook National Park is home to the majority of New Zealand's only International Dark Sky Reserve.

This region has been labelled as one of the best stargazing sites on Earth, which says something for our little country at the bottom of the world. Mt Cook hosts some of the darkest skies in the world.

Book yourself on a Big Sky Stargazing Tour. The experienced guides will introduce you to the beautiful Southern Sky with a full hour viewing with the naked eye, Astro-binoculars, and state of the art 14" and 11" astronomy telescopes. View the southern cross, seasonal ecliptic objects, planets, and stunning star clusters. See moons, distant galaxies, and the Milky Way. Even the weather is no barrier to this magnificent spatial beauty with viewing in the Planetarium indoors.

Mountain Walks

There are 10 short walks that begin near the Mt Cook village. All tracks are formed and well-marked, such as Governors Bush walk, Bowen Bush Walk, and Glencoe Walk for gentle meanders through New Zealand bush to a Look-out point.

For more adventurous alpine hikers, there are 3 mountain pass routes, Mueller, Copland, and Bull passes.

Glacier Viewing and Skiing

Helicopters and ski-planes provide access to the majestic glaciers'. The Tasman glacier is an excellent choice for intermediate skiers, while the Murchison, Darwin and Bonney Glaciers offer more excitement for advanced skiers. From October to May you can explore the Tasman Glacier's terminal lake by boat.

Mountaineering

Climbing Mt Cook remains the eternal challenge, however there are many other peaks to tempt experienced climbers, Tasman, Malte Brun, Elie de Beaumont, Sefton, and La Perouse are the local favourite climbing haunts.

Climbers don't require permits but are requested to complete a trips intention form at the Department of Conservation Visitor Centre. Local guides are available for climbing, walking and glacier skiing.

Winter climbing is an extreme sport, only recommended for well-prepared, experienced mountaineers. The Park has an airport serving domestic commercial flights and scenic flight operators.

The weather can change very quickly – be prepared for heavy rainfall, snow, and/or high winds.

Accommodation

The Department of Conservation provides 17 huts in the park. Most are positioned to provide accommodation for Mountaineers, and you need climbing skills to reach them. Non-climbing visitors can enjoy the attractions of

Mt Cook village which offers everything from Backpackers to Luxury Hotels.

The nearest towns are Twizel and Lake Tekapo offering a range of restaurants, cafes, and accommodation.

As an end of Holiday splurge try a night in The Hermitage Hotel right in the heart of Mt Cook village and enjoy all your meals in warmth and comfort.

These are 3 of the jewels from the New Zealand National Park Crown. These are the most popular National Parks in New Zealand. There is so much to see, do and experience in these natural playgrounds.

Price List for Activities & Accommodation

Big Sky Stargazing Tours $78.00 Adult

The Hermitage Hotel From $255.00 pn Adult

Conclusion

As this guide concludes, you will have learned the basics of sounding like a local, how, and where to find wallet friendly places to lay your head and how to live on the smell of an oily rag, food wise.

We have danced the length and breadth of the country, looked at the settlement history and the indigenous people of the land. Looked at outlying spots you need to catch ferries or helicopters to visit.

With this guide you get bang for your buck with recipes included to make the best of your seafood odyssey. You have learned some fun facts of this land down under.

Additional information around environment and how you as the traveller can contribute before and through your trip. Information that made it into the guide as an afterthought or as a "Ahh, they need know about this." As things have come to mind and memories resurfaced.

I have had a wonderful time, walking you through my country via the guide. Showing you New Zealand hospitality through the lens of a different culture. Saying, excitedly to you, "Hey, come and look at this!" "Don't forget to try this!" Researching to find the cheapest way for you to get around while staying eco-friendly.

It is not possible to see everything in one trip. You won't need any excuse to come back and see more and experience more delights. I often tell people, New Zealand is a country you should visit at least once, and I still say this, however I also add, come back to see what you missed the last time and keep coming back until you have done and seen it all.

For travellers, whose visas make it possible, you can work and travel for 12 months, so why wouldn't you. Imagine waking up in these lush surrounds every day, making lifelong friends along the way.

One of the sayings I grew up with, was "Don't leave home until you have seen the country." As I was writing, I was writing to myself too, as I realized, I had not seen all of the country and as a result I am planning a trip to Stewart Island. Waiheke Island is in my sights for near the end of the year. I am also looking at a trip to Queenstown.

There have been times throughout, where commentary has been serious, particularly when describing some of New Zealand's tragic events. Keeping yourself and your friends safe while travelling. Warning of natural and man-made disasters. While these things do happen, they are not a daily threat. It is still important that you know the possibilities and what happens when disaster strikes.

Environmentally, we have discovered the impacts on the land of both man-made and natural disasters. The clean-up bill and the cost to the land is high.

Now, that borders in New Zealand are open again, this is a beginning. Start your travels here in New Zealand, take mirids of photos to show back home and next time bring your friends or family.

You can set your own itinerary; this guide has shown

you the possibilities. You can design your own path through New Zealand while following all the relevant rules, laws, and regulations. Make New Zealand more than a bucket list dream, plan and make it happen.

You have seen though this guide the colorful vibrancy that awaits you here, the glittering cities, and the clear night skies, the heart stopping adventures, and the lazy relaxed beach days. The sightseeing, the camping and glamping and don't forget the wildlife sightings.

New Zealander's learn cultural norms from you too, you show us yours and we will show you ours.

The only item left is to offer you an open invitation to come and enjoy your time here. Welcome, stay a while, relax, and tell your friends back home about New Zealand, Land of the long white cloud and extend the invitation to them with our complements.

All prices quoted are subject to change without notice. Activities advertised may change without notice.